In My Mother's *Mind*

A MEMOIR

DIANE ZELLA

Copyright © 2023 Diane Zella.

All rights reserved. No part of this book may be reproduced, stored, or transmitted by any means—whether auditory, graphic, mechanical, or electronic—without written permission of both publisher and author, except in the case of brief excerpts used in critical articles and reviews. Unauthorized reproduction of any part of this work is illegal and is punishable by law.

ISBN: 979-8-89031-258-7 (sc)
ISBN: 979-8-89031-259-4 (hc)
ISBN: 979-8-89031-260-0 (e)

Because of the dynamic nature of the Internet, any web addresses or links contained in this book may have changed since publication and may no longer be valid. The views expressed in this work are solely those of the author and do not necessarily reflect the views of the publisher, and the publisher hereby disclaims any responsibility for them.

One Galleria Blvd., Suite 1900, Metairie, LA 70001
1-888-421-2397

To the Reader,

Thank you for choosing In My Mother's Mind: A Memoir. You were constantly on my mind as I wrote this book. If you are struggling to care for someone with dementia, I pray you will be inspired and helped by my story. I truly empathize with your struggle and know how hard this is for you. If I have provided you any comfort, then I've accomplished my goal.

Diane

For Lynn and Jimmy

ACKNOWLEDGMENTS

Foremost, I want to thank God for giving me the inspiration, motivation, and determination to write this book. He is always the constant in my life.

My sister Carol for surviving the journey with our mother with me. Carol has always had my back from the day I was born, and I know I would never have made it through this life without her.

Special acknowledgment to Carol's spouse, Pete. Although he is no longer with us, he was a rock for me throughout my life. Just surviving his mother-in-law for over fifty years is beyond all comprehension.

My uncle Ray and aunt Charlotte, who are no longer with us. They selflessly gave their time to help take Mom to doctor's appointments so I wouldn't have to miss too much work.

My children, Lynn and Jimmy, for always being willing to help with Grandma whenever I needed it. I know she wasn't an easy person to be around, but I very much appreciate the effort.

Mary Foreman, who read the manuscript before it went to the publisher, providing me with valuable feedback. My husband, Ben, for always supporting my dreams.

INTRODUCTION

When I was thrown into the world of dementia and caring for my mother, I did not go willingly. I went kicking and screaming the entire way. Just ask God. He'll tell you how many times I raged at him. Once I settled down to my new reality, however, I tried my best to care for Mother lovingly. Mother didn't make it easy. Throughout the process, I realized other people might benefit from the things I learned throughout this process, and the idea for this book was born.

Probably the best thing you can do for yourself is gather a support system. You have to have someone to talk to and share your frustrations. My support group consisted of God and my family. I was always afraid of overwhelming them, but they were always reassuring and loving to me. Please take care of yourself as you care for your loved one.

PROLOGUE

Waiting behind the wheel of the pickup truck, the Florida sun felt warm on my face. I closed my eyes, and my mind wondered to the events of the past week. I wish I could have gotten to the beach just one day, but there was too much work to do. I still couldn't believe what we accomplished this week. All my mother's belongings were safely packed in the U-Haul in front of me. As I opened my eyes for one last look at the mobile home I will never visit again, a small pang of sorrow touched my heart. Pulling me out of my reverie, I heard the sound of my mother and my sister arguing. I looked in the rearview mirror to see them standing in the middle of the road.

Slowly, I opened the driver's door, put my feet on the pavement, and turned to see what all the ruckus is about.

"If I can't drive, I'm not going!" shouted my mother.

My sister responded, "But, Mother, we have this all settled. I'm going to drive your car until we return the rental truck. Then Diane will drive your car, and I will ride in the U-Haul with Pete."

"NO! I am going to drive my own car. I still know how to drive, you know."

Looking at me for help, my sister threw up her hands, turned, and walked to the U-Haul. Now what do I do? Mother got into her car and sat with clenched hands on the steering wheel while I'm left standing alone in the street. I walked forward to the U-Haul, and Pete rolled down the window.

"Change of plans," I said. "Since she refuses to let Carol drive her car, all we can do is let her drive to the airport. At the airport, I will try to talk some sense into her. We will put her between you and me. I'll start out, Mother will follow, and you bring up the rear." Pete nodded silently.

Next, I walked to the rear to talk to Mother. She reluctantly rolled down her window. "I am going to lead, and you will follow me. Pete will be right behind you in the U-Haul. We have to stop at the airport so I can turn in the rental truck before we get on the road."

With a small "okay," Mom rolled up her window, and I got back into the rental truck. Once the seat belt was buckled, I said yet another prayer that God will see us all safely to the airport, and I turned the truck north to begin the next phase of the journey. How in the world did we get here? Things have moved so quickly that my head is spinning. Can I really handle what I have signed up for?

"God help me," I whispered.

PART I

ONE

Ohio was enjoying an exceptional fall. All the windows in the condo were open, and I was relaxing on my patio with a book and a glass of tea. I liked to spend quiet Sundays before plunging back into a hectic workweek. But then the phone rang, disturbing my peace.

"Hello?"

"Hi! Did I wake you up?" an overly cheerful voice sang on the other end of the line.

"No. It's the middle of the afternoon, Mom. I was sitting on the patio," I said as I rolled my eyes.

"Oh. You sounded sleepy. Anyway, I called to tell you I'm coming to Ohio for Thanksgiving. I was able to get a direct flight into Dayton on Saturday, the twentieth."

"Okay." When my head stopped spinning, I guess I had to be thankful she was at least giving me a six-week notice. "I'll pick you up at the airport."

"You don't have to pick me up. I'm renting a car and driving myself."

"Mom, you really don't have to do that. You can save the money on the rental car, and I'll be happy to pick you up."

"No, I want to rent a car. I'll visit with Raymond and maybe some of my Eastern Star friends while you are at work. This way, I can come and go as I please, and you don't have to drive me around."

"It's really no trouble. I'm sure we can work something out. I just don't think you need to rent a car."

"This is what I want to do, and that's the end of the discussion." Once again, I've been put in my place. End of discussion.

"Okay. Well, then, I guess we'll see you on the twentieth."

Now to rethink Thanksgiving. I had already asked Ben's sister, Anna, to join us. Adding another place setting to the table was not the problem. Mother just wasn't very good at being social, and making "new friends" was not her particular forte. Anna was an introvert to the tenth power and not good at meeting new people either. I envisioned the two of them sitting across the room and staring at each other. With any luck, I could keep Mother engaged, and Ben could handle his sister. Besides, Thanksgiving is supposed to be full of drama, isn't it?

When my kids heard the news, they were less than enthusiastic as well. Out of five grandchildren, Mother had two favorites. The other grandkids were just out of luck when it came to attention from her. However, one of her favorites happened to be my son because he was the only boy. This meant she would at least be civil to him, and all I had to do was try to keep my daughter close to me. Thankfully, she would have to work after school every day until Thanksgiving. The distance would help tremendously.

Next, I talked to Ben and explained the situation. As always, he was understanding and confident that it would not be a problem. He would help in any way to ease the undoubted tension during the event. I am so blessed to have him in my life.

Now, where is the air mattress? I thought as I climbed the stairs to my bedroom. She could have the bed, and I'll take the air mattress. I'm not going to make the kids give up their beds. I would have to spend the next six weeks cleaning my son's bedroom in order to make it livable for Grandma. Besides, he had a waterbed, and I knew she would not sleep on it. My daughter's bedroom floor was just normally littered with shoes and clothes but still was not a good option given the animosity between Lynn and her grandmother. Why does it always have to be so difficult? I'm worn-out already, and she isn't even here yet!

Scavenging through the linen closet, I found no air mattress. Perhaps I put it in my closet. No luck there either. Only one place left. Yes! The coat closet was the winner. I took the mattress upstairs. With that done, I think I deserve to return to my peaceful patio and replace my tea with a glass of wine. Only six weeks until D-Day.

TWO

Six weeks seemed to fly by. When you are a single mom with two teenagers, the pace of life is quite hectic. November 20 snuck up on me, and now it was time to go into overdrive. I opened the kids' bedroom doors and cheerfully chirped, "Rise and shine!" Neither of them, of course, was very cheerful or sunny.

"Come on, you guys, get up. We have a lot of work to do before Grandma gets here. We need to make the house as presentable as possible. I don't want to give her any more ammunition than she's already carrying with her."

"What time does she get here?" asked my daughter sullenly.

"I figure she should be here around two. Let's get started on the downstairs. We can always close your bedroom doors if we aren't able to get them cleaned by then."

All of us trudged downstairs to begin picking up the clutter, running the vacuum, dusting, and cleaning the kitchen along with the downstairs bathroom. By noon, the downstairs looked good. I didn't get the baseboards dusted, I thought to myself. She could pick on that if she couldn't find anything else. She always did when I was a kid anyway. It really didn't matter how hard I worked to clean the place; she would find something wrong.

With two hours to go, I headed upstairs to my room. All it needed was a good sweeping and then to clean my bathroom. I sent the kids to their bathroom to attempt cleaning in there. Two teenagers could certainly destroy a bathroom. After inflating the air mattress and fitting it with sheets, I thought there were few things she would find to complain about.

She should be here any minute, I thought. I'll just throw a load of laundry into the washer and think about what to have for dinner.

Two o'clock came and went and still no Mother. Maybe she was caught up in traffic. Getting through Dayton traffic could have slowed her up. I wish she'd have let me pick her up, I thought to myself. What if she's been in an accident? What if she got off the wrong exit and doesn't know where she is? The area looks so much different from the last time she drove here. Has she even ever driven from the airport to my house before? I couldn't remember her making that trip.

As the hands on the clock passed four, my imagination was running wild. She's never had a cell phone and wouldn't know how to use it if she did have one. With no way to contact her and anxiety flooding my entire body, I decided to start dinner to distract myself. At four thirty, the doorbell rang, and my heart was in my throat. Walking the hallway, I prepared myself for the police officer I knew must be on the other side of the door; I opened it to find my mother standing on the step. She stepped across the threshold as if nothing was out of the ordinary. I hugged her and asked, "Was your plane delayed?"

"No. Why?"

"Mom, you should have been here two and a half hours ago. What happened?"

"Nothing happened. Why are you so upset?"

"I'm upset because it took you four and a half hours to drive from the airport to my house. I can make the trip in an hour, but I factored in extra time for you. Why did it take so long?"

"I was just driving. I guess I don't drive as fast as other people."

Exasperated, I hung her coat in the closet and led her to the living room. Calling up the stairs, I asked my son to carry her things in from the car.

"Please just put everything in my room, and we'll sort it out later," I told him. "Thanks."

Rejoining Mother in the living room, I asked if she was hungry. Dinner was almost ready. While I finished up in the kitchen, she moved herself to the dining table and regaled me with the mundane events happening in the mobile home park where she lived in Florida. Most of this was news I already knew because it never changed much from one conversation to another.

My daughter arrived in the kitchen having just emerged from the shower.

"Hi, Grandma. Did you have a good trip?"

"My trip was fine, but your mother is all mad about something. She said it took me too long to get here from the airport. I can see what kind of visit this is going to be."

"I'm sure she was just worried about you is all."

"That figures. Take her side."

As my daughter rolled her eyes, I asked her to please set the table so we could eat. Dinner was mostly a silent affair. I was still cooling off and couldn't think of much to say. Thankfully, the kids talked a little about school, and my daughter talked about some of the kids in her swim classes. We muddled through the evening with some television and an early bedtime.

Sunday morning, we were readying for church when Mother announced she didn't want to go. She doesn't like my church much.

"There's all that getting up and down, and then they make you shake hands with other people."

"It's called 'sharing the peace,' Mom. It's a way of greeting other Christians and offering them the peace of the Lord."

"I don't care. It's not my cup of tea. I'll just wait for you here. I brought along some knitting, and I'll work on that."

"Fine. I'll fix breakfast when I get home. There is coffee in the pot on the counter. Mugs are in the cabinet above it. We should be home by ten."

I prayed all the way to church, during church, and coming home from church. I'm sure God's ears were on fire. I needed his peace big-time, and I would need Herculean help to get through this week. My weekly prayer group was wrapping me in prayer. They knew the challenges I had with my mother. My sister and her family were also continuously praying. They knew better than anyone did what I was going to be dealing with.

Falling into bed felt like falling into the arms of Jesus. I knew I was going to be okay. God had me.

THREE

Monday dawned dreary and drizzly. However, this rainy Monday wasn't going to get me down. I only had to work two days this week and was looking forward to some time off even it meant spending the days with my mom. I asked Mom what she was going to do with herself while I was at work and the kids were at school.

"I thought I might drive to Miamisburg to see your uncle Ray. I also thought I'd try to find a Hallmark store to buy a card. Lynn's birthday is coming up, isn't it?"

"As a matter of fact, it's today," I said. "I'm picking up a cake at the grocery store after work, and we'll have a little celebration with dinner. Ben and Michael are going to join us as well."

"So you aren't going to make her cake, huh?"

"Mom, it has been a little busy around here lately. I have to work, and then I have to cook Thanksgiving dinner for twelve people. Lynn knows how hard it is having a birthday on or around Thanksgiving."

"You always had to make her cakes when she was little. Store-bought wasn't good enough for you."

"I was a stay-home mom then. I'm a working single mom now. I don't have much free time anymore. Anyway, I don't have time to stand here arguing with you. I need to drop the kids at school and get to work. There is a Hallmark store just down the street. Turn left out of the driveway, make another left at the stop sign, and just stay on Main Street. The store is in Colony Square shopping center about two miles from here. Do you need directions to Uncle Ray's?"

"I know how to get to Ray's house. I've been there a million times."

"Okay. Well, be careful and have a good day. The kids should be home around three, and I will be home about six. Bye."

For some reason, Mondays in law offices are quite hectic. Once I got to the office, Mother was the furthest thing from my mind. Around three, my phone rang. My son had just gotten home from school and was calling. "How was your day?"

"It was okay. Where's Grandma?"

"Your guess is as good as mine. She said she was going to the Hallmark store and then going to Miamisburg to see Uncle Ray. I'm sure she'll be back soon. She might have gone out for lunch with Ray and Charlotte. I need to get back to work so I can leave on time. Talk to you when I get home."

Pulling into the driveway at the end of the day, I was relieved to see the rental car in the parking space. I couldn't believe she found her way back. I didn't know what I was so worried about. My son met me at the door and helped to carry the cake in.

"I see Grandma made it back okay."

"Well, she made it back, but I don't know if it's okay."

"What are you talking about?"

"She didn't get here until after four. She didn't go to Uncle Ray's."

"Where in the heck did she go?"

"To the Hallmark store."

"Oh. She must have decided to stay here then."

I hung up my coat and made my way to the kitchen to start dinner. Ben and Michael would be here any minute, bringing Lynn home from the YMCA where she worked.

"Hi, Mom. How was your day?"

"It was okay."

"Did you get any more knitting done today?"

"Who had time for that? It took me all afternoon to find the Hallmark store. It wasn't where you said it would be. I drove all over town and finally found it."

In astonishment, I said, "It's two miles down the road. What do you mean you drove all over town?"

"I guess I got turned around. I don't know."

"So I guess you didn't see Uncle Ray."

"Well, I didn't have time after it took so long to buy the damn card."

"How about we all go see him this weekend? I'll drive."

"I guess so."

As I turned, Ben came through the door with Michael and the birthday girl.

"There she is! Happy birthday!"

"Thanks, Mom."

"Have you been having a good day?"

"It's been okay."

"Dinner's almost ready. Everyone, wash your hands. Jimmy, would you please set the table?"

Thanks to everyone else at the table, conversation was lively while Mother sulked. Lynn enjoyed birthday cake, presents, and cards. She rounded the table and tried to give Mother a hug, which was hard to do when someone won't stand up to reciprocate.

"Thank you for the card, Grandma."

"Uh-huh."

"Thank you, Ben and Michael, for the card and money," she said as she approached them and gave hugs.

Of course, these hugs were better received and freely given in return. Would it really have taken very much effort for my mother to do the same? I don't know why I'm surprised, but I always remain hopeful. As we all had school and work the next day, it was an early evening. We said our goodbyes and headed upstairs to bed. I gave the kids extra-long hugs and said "I love you," trying to make up for the indifference expressed by Mom. I wanted to yell at her, "These are your grandchildren!" I didn't. Instead, we discussed the next day.

"So do you have anything planned for tomorrow while I'm at work?"

"Oh, I think I'll just stay here and piddle around. I've got enough to keep me busy."

"Okay. I think that might be a good idea. I'll see if I can leave work a little early, depending on what my boss has going on. I want to get started on some of the prep work for the meal on Thursday. Maybe you can help me."

"We'll see."

"Or I'll just do it myself. No big deal," I said as I turned out the light and rolled over to sleep.

FOUR

For as long as I can remember, I yearned for family. My sister, Carol, is seventeen years older than I am, so I grew up as an only child. Because my mother had me at the ripe old age of thirty-six, my parents were older than those of my friends'. Much of my growing up was spent alone or with adults. My sister married when I was four, and her first child was born when I was six. My nieces became more like siblings to me, and my sister was more of a mom to me than a sister. Growing up, holiday meals were mostly just my parents and me. My sister and her family generally spent holidays with her husband's family. I remembered being jealous of my nieces when they talked of the fun they had playing with their cousins. I wanted that. I wanted to be part of a bigger family. Instead, I settled for every opportunity I could get to stay at my sister's house.

At my sister's house, Carol always spent time with me even if it was only to play games at the kitchen table while she was doing the weekly ironing. Other times, she let me play in her kitchen using dishes and pans, pretending like I was cooking! When my nieces were older, we spent the long summer days dreaming up adventures in the backyard. Maybe there were difficult times at my sister's house, but I only remember all the wonderfulness. I looked up to Carol and wanted to be just like her when I grew up. Most of all, I wanted a family just like hers when I grew up.

When I married my first husband, I thought that dream had finally come true. He had four siblings and more aunts, uncles, and cousins than I ever imagined. Holiday meals with his family were extraordinary to me. Once my brothers-in-law started having families, I cherished having twenty people at my house for Thanksgiving! When we divorced, I was back to having three. A Thanksgiving table of three was very depressing to me, so I worked on building my family again.

Now, I included other single parents who would otherwise be alone for Thanksgiving. Thanksgiving had always been my favorite holiday, and I was going to move forward keeping the traditions I established and including people who were important to me. In keeping with this custom, a widow and her two children became a staple at our Thanksgiving table. Lori and I met at church before her husband died. He died when the children were three and five. Lori's family lived out of town and gathered on the weekend after Thanksgiving, leaving her little family alone on Thanksgiving Day. They were always welcome at my table.

On this particular Thanksgiving, my table was to be full again with the inclusion of Mother, my significant other, Ben, his sister, Anna, and his son, Michael, Lori and her children and my children. My heart was full, and we were blessed. This mindset was how I chose to start my Thanksgiving celebration. The house was a bustle with the food preparation and table setup. My kids were a great help while my mother watched the Macy's parade from a comfy chair in the living room. I didn't mind. Sometimes, it was easier to have her not helping.

All the guests began arriving around two, and the house was filling with delicious smells, lively conversation, and laughter. The older kids entertained the younger ones. Most of the adults chattered about the normal nonsense of everyday life. Then there was Mother and Ben's sister, Anna. They sat in the living room, separated from the other adults (at their own choice), eyeing each other suspiciously. Any attempt to pull them into the conversation was met with either stony silence or short, non-conversational answers. Eventually, I stopped trying and just allowed them to sit in their quiet corners ignoring everyone and everything around them.

After dinner, the kids had a tradition of watching Home Alone, so it wasn't long before the smallest child was asking to start the movie. The adults settled into soft couches and chairs while the kids sprawled on the floor.

Anna said she was getting a migraine and needed to leave before the headache got any worse.

"Thank you for having me," she said at the door.

"I'm so glad you were able to join us, and I hope you will come again." She never did.

When the movie had finished, Lori rounded up her kids, and they left too. Ben and I returned to living room after saying goodbyes. Jimmy and Michael sat on the floor to play. Michael brought out his box of Pokémon cards, and the two of them spent time perusing his collection. The adults were enjoying another cup of coffee when Mother blurted out, "He stole a twenty-dollar bill from my purse."

Shocked and horrified, I asked, "What in the world are you talking about?"

"Michael. He stole that $20 from my purse."

Looking at Michael's box, I saw the $20. However, it certainly was not unusual for Michael to have money.

Michael received money gifts from relatives and was good at saving it. I had seen Michael with money before.

"Mother, before you go accusing someone of stealing, shouldn't you have some evidence?"

"I know that's my $20."

"How do you know that?"

Mom retrieved her purse and opened her billfold. I saw a ten and some ones.

"Do you see a twenty-dollar bill there?"

"No. But I also don't know if you had a twenty-dollar bill to begin with."

"Are you calling me a liar?"

"I'm not calling you a liar, but I do wonder if maybe you are mistaken. I've never known Michael to steal anything, let alone go into someone's purse or wallet and steal money."

"Oh, I see. You're going to believe him because he's your boyfriend's son."

"Mother!" Turning to Ben and Michael, I apologized and asked for their forgiveness.

Ben took Michael from the room and asked him about the $20 in his box and where he had gotten it. Michael explained it was money he was saving to buy more Pokémon cards and vehemently denied stealing it. Ben believed him as did I.

"Mother, you owe both Ben and Michael an apology. Now."

"Sorry."

"That's not much of an apology, but I guess it's all we are going to get."

Ben asked Michael to gather his things as it was time they should be going anyway. It was getting late, and Michael needed to get to bed. We said our goodbyes at the front door, and I returned to the living room. Angrily, I confronted my mother.

"I have never been so humiliated in my life," I said to her. Thinking back on it, there definitely were other times when my mother had humiliated me in front of others, but I was going for effect here.

"I cannot believe that you insulted my guests in such a horrific way."

"Well, I don't care what any of you say. Michael did steal that money."

"Mother, isn't it possible that you gave a twenty-dollar bill to the clerk at the Hallmark store when you bought Lynn's card?"

"No, I didn't."

"How did you buy the card?"

"I paid cash."

"How much cash did you have?"

"I don't remember." She had a puzzled look on her face as her argument crumbled around her.

"Do you think you could have perhaps jumped to a wrong conclusion when you saw Michael's $20?"

"Probably not. You just can't trust kids, and I've always thought he looks a little cagey."

"Okay. We're done here. Michael did not steal that money, and we are not carrying on this conversation. Come on, everyone, off to bed."

My kids, stunned by what had just transpired, quietly made their way to their bedrooms. I turned off the lights, checked the door locks, and stopped in each child's room to tell them good night. My daughter whispered in the dark, "Mom, how could she say those things about Michael?"

"I don't know, sweetie. She has never had a very high opinion of children, but I've never seen her do that before."

My son, Jimmy, came to the door and whispered, "Mom, I was with Michael all day, and I never saw him go anywhere near Grandma's purse."

"I know, Jimmy. Thank you for saying that. I'm not completely sure what is happening with Grandma, but something isn't right. She's been forgetful before, but her behavior so far this week has been bizarre."

Contemplating my words, I closed their bedroom doors and headed toward mine. Settling down in bed, the only thing I could think to do was pray. As my ex-husband used to ridicule me, that's how I handle everything. I thanked God that's how I handle everything. I didn't know how else I would have made it through my life. I also asked God to open my eyes to see what was happening with Mother and what I needed to do to help her.

FIVE

The remainder of Mother's visit was fairly uneventful. On Friday, as is my custom, I dragged out the Christmas decorations, put up the tree, and decorated the house. "Mom, would you like to help decorate the tree?"

"No," she said quietly.

"Is everything all right?"

"I'm fine."

She didn't look fine, but I dropped it and carried on with my decorating. I hoped she would tell me when she was ready. Saturday, we went to visit Uncle Ray and Aunt Charlotte. I probably hadn't seen them in a year (as was normal), and we had much to catch up on. Throughout the couple of hours we were there, Mother hardly said two words. She seemed to be sulking, but I couldn't figure out why. She had been adamant about seeing her brother, but now she wasn't even talking to him.

Eventually, we said our goodbyes with hugs, "I love yous," and promises to get together again soon. In the car, I tried to pull Mother out of the stupor she seemed to be in.

"That was a nice visit. You didn't seem to have much to say."

"How could I get a word in edgewise?" Mother asked incredulously. "Charlotte wouldn't shut up long enough to give me a chance to talk to Raymond. She never has liked me. She's always trying to come between me and Ray."

Trying to keep one eye on the road to avoid an accident, I quickly glanced Mother's direction to see if maybe she was joking. She was not. Her mouth was set in a thin line, and her arms were crossed over her chest.

"Mom, I'm not sure what you mean. Aunt Charlotte barely talked unless it was to answer someone's question."

"There you go again. Taking the other person's side against me. What did I ever do to you to cause such animosity?"

Well, that was a loaded question, but I wasn't about to get into that now. Do I let that comment drop, or do I carry the topic forward? Thankfully, my son spoke up just then.

"Mom, can we see if the Hamburger Wagon is open? We haven't gone there for a long time."

"Sure. Let's go see."

The Hamburger Wagon is an icon in the town where I grew up. It's just a little horse-drawn wagon that parks on the city square and sells hamburgers. That's all they sell, but they are the best burgers in the world. People come from miles around. As we approached the square, the line of cars was at least six deep, but it was worth the wait. When I brought the little white bag back to the car, we all dove in. The hamburger seemed to be turning Mother's mood around, and we quietly drove the forty-five minutes home.

Still perplexed by Mother's behavior, we all prepared for bed. The same discussion ensued about church the next day, but I received the same answer. No. She didn't want to go to church with us.

Sunday greeted us with clouds and a chill in the air. Mother was flying back to Florida on Monday, and I was more than ready for this weekend to be over. Sunday afternoon, we watched a movie together and began preparations for a dinner of Thanksgiving leftovers. Mother was just picking at her food.

"Are you not hungry?"

"I don't have much of an appetite."

"Are you feeling ill?"

"No."

"I bet you're excited to be going home tomorrow, huh? Back to the nice warm Florida sunshine?"

"I don't want to go back to Florida."

"Excuse me?"

"I want to move back to Ohio."

Mom had lived in Florida for twenty-two years. She retired at sixty-two with the minimum Social Security benefit and a paltry pension from the place where she had worked for twenty-five years. She sold the house in Ohio, packed up her belongings, and left. Her father had lived near Orlando, Florida, and we visited him every year in August until he died. Even after he died, we took summer vacations in Florida. Mother's dream was to one day live there herself. She made her dream come true.

She moved into a mobile home park filled with other retirees. Mother never looked her age, and at age sixtytwo, she was spry as ever. She learned to play golf and tennis. She joined a bowling league! I didn't know who this person was, but it sure wasn't my mother. The residents of the park held dances and bicycle parades. They were always celebrating something, and Mother was right there in the thick of it with them. She was having the time of her life, and I was very glad. Having her a thousand miles away made for a much better relationship. She had her life, and I had mine.

However, there was one little drawback. Mom wasn't quite as free as the other retirees in the park were. Her Social Security and pension checks barely gave her enough money to pay the bills. She had to work to supplement her income and was still working at age eighty. I only hoped I had her stamina and good health when I was her age.

Given all this history, I could not understand why she was telling me now that she wanted to move back to Ohio. There really wasn't anything here for her anymore. All the ties she had to Ohio, except for family, were broken when she moved. Her life now was in Florida.

"What are you talking about, Mom? You love Florida."

"I want to move back to Ohio."

"Has something happened? Are you scared?"

"Nothing has happened. I just don't want to live there anymore. All my friends have died or are dying. I want to be near family again."

You could have pushed me over with a feather. Family had never been anything my mother wanted to be around. She had spent her whole life trying to get away from us, and now she's telling me she wanted to be nearer.

Did I just step into a parallel universe somehow? Shaking my head to clear the fog, I was finally able to respond.

"Are you sure about this? Have you thought it through?"

"I'm sure. I don't want to go back tomorrow."

"Um, Mom, you have to go back tomorrow. You can't just stay here and leave everything in Florida. You have a lot of loose ends we will need to tie up before you can move back. It isn't something that can be done in a day. We have to think this through and make plans. Do you want me to take you to the airport tomorrow?"

"No. I've got to turn in the rental car. I can manage."

"You're sure?"

"Yes."

"Okay. I will make a list of everything we need to do, and then we can figure out the timing on this. After you get home, I'll give you a call after I've had time to process the information."

Lying in bed that night, I had a hard time getting to sleep. Good grief! How was I supposed to handle this news? We were going to have to sell her mobile home and move everything back to Ohio. I was going to need to find housing for her here but had no idea where to start with that. I finally got to sleep sometime after midnight and woke groggily to the alarm. Somehow, I had to get through the day at work and hope to get to bed early.

With coffee in hand, I rushed the kids into the car. Mom's suitcase was sitting by the front door, and I offered to load it into the rental car before I left.

"No. I can get it."

"It will only take a minute. How about if I ask Jimmy to run it out for you?"

"Oh, all right."

Jimmy put the suitcase in the trunk of the car and hopped into my car. We waved goodbye to Mom and headed off to work and school. I looked in the rearview window to see Mother forlornly waving from the front door. A feeling of trepidation settled in my stomach. All I could do was hope she made it home safely and said a prayer to that effect.

In the afternoon, I received a call at work from my son.

"Mom."

"Hi, buddy. How was school?"

"Mom."

"What's the matter?"

"It's Grandma."

"Did she call? Did she get home okay?"

"Mom. She's still here. When I got home from school, I found her sitting in her car in the parking lot. She said she'd been sitting there all day."

"She what!"

"She said she locked herself out of the house and couldn't get back in so she just sat in the car." I hung up the phone and cradled my head in my hands. My boss walked up to my desk.

"Are you okay?"

"No. I'm not. My mother was supposed to fly back to Florida this morning, but she never made it to the airport. My son just called. Apparently, she has been sitting in her rental car in my parking lot all day. I think I need to leave and get this straightened out."

"Okay. Did you get those revisions done to the purchase agreement I gave you?"

"It's on your desk."

"Did you finish that tape of dictation I left you after lunch?"

"On your chair."

"Is there anything else out here that needs to be finished before you leave?"

"Fred, everything is done. There's a little filing, but that can certainly wait until tomorrow."

"All right, you can go."

I gathered my things and headed out the door before he had a chance to change his mind. I knew there was a Delta service counter in the lobby of the building next to where I worked. I guess the look on my face gave me away as the airline representative asked me if I was okay.

"Well, not really. My mother was supposed to be on Flight 6682 this morning from Dayton to Tampa, and she missed it. Do I have to buy an entirely new ticket for her?"

"Let's take a look. I think we can just move her to another flight, and you will only have to pay the change fee."

"Oh, that would be awesome."

"Okay. I see her ticket here. When would you like the next flight? We have one leaving tonight at 6:00 p.m."

"That doesn't give me enough time to go get her and get back to the airport. What do you have for tomorrow?"

"We have a flight tomorrow at 9:00 a.m., if that would work."

"That would be perfect. I can drop her off on my way to work."

"All right. Would she like an aisle or window seat?"

"Let's put her by the window."

"I'll just need $50 for the change fee."

I handed her my credit card and breathed a sigh of relief. A thought popped into my head unexpectedly.

"Would it be possible to get some help for her once she gets to the airport? Would there be anyone who could make sure she gets on the airplane? She is eighty years old, and I think she is a little confused."

"We do have a concierge service for senior passengers. Does she need a wheelchair?"

"Oh no. Nothing like that. She would have a fit if she knew I was even asking for help for her, so we need to keep it low-key. I can get her to her gate, if someone could take over from there."

"We can do that. I am making a note in the computer now. You are all set. I hope everything works out for you."

"Thank you so much. You have been a lifesaver. Thank you."

On my way to the parking garage to retrieve my car, I remembered that Mother's friend, Val, was supposed to pick her up at the airport in Tampa. I quickly looked through the contacts on my cell phone but found nothing there. I then called the house, and my son answered the phone. I asked him to look at my personal phone book by the phone and give me the number for Val. Thankfully, he was able to find it. Val answered on the third ring.

"Hello?"

"Hi, Val. This is Ethel's daughter, Diane."

"Oh my gosh. I'm so glad to hear from you. Is your mom okay? I waited at the airport for over an hour, and she never appeared."

"I'm so sorry you had to drive all that way. Yes. She's okay. She missed her flight, but I didn't find out until about an hour ago. I have her booked on a 9:00 a.m. flight tomorrow morning. She has a layover in Atlanta, but she is supposed to land in Tampa at 12:05 p.m. I hate to ask you again to pick her up. Is there anyone else I can call?"

"Nonsense. I'll pick her up. I don't mind at all. I was hoping that was all that was wrong. I'm glad to know it was just because she missed her flight. Tell her I'll be at the airport at noon tomorrow. Thanks for calling."

Upon arriving at home, I found Mom sitting at the dining table fidgeting with the tablecloth. She looked so small all of a sudden. For as long as I could remember, Mother always appeared larger than life. This is not a compliment. It just meant that she was always in control of everything. Mostly, it was her way or the highway. She was never interested in your advice or your opinion. She had been taking care of herself from a young age, and she didn't need anything from anyone. Now, however, she looked sad and fearful.

I sat down opposite her and told her about the arrangements I'd made for her to fly out in the morning.

"Your flight leaves at 9:00 a.m., which gives me plenty of time to get you to the airport and then get to the office on time. I am going to drive the rental car, and Lynn is going to drive my car. I will turn in the rental and take you and your bags to the gate."

"You don't need to take me to the gate. I can get there myself."

"I'm not so sure. This will just give me some peace of mind." She glared at me but agreed.

"Would you like me to have a flight attendant help you on the plane?" I asked.

"What? Do you think I'm a child? I'm perfectly capable of getting on an airplane."

"After this morning, I'm not sure what you are capable of anymore. What happened? Jimmy said he found you sitting in the car in the parking lot when he came home from school."

"Well, I was ready to go to the airport. I got in the car and realized I forgot something in the house. The door was locked, and I couldn't get in, so I just had to wait for someone to come home."

"What did you forget?"

"I can't remember now."

Slumping in my chair, the light bulb went off in my head. This was much worse than I thought. She had in her mind that she didn't want to go back to Florida, so she sabotaged her departure. Either that or she was afraid to drive back to the airport because she couldn't remember the way. The travel between Florida and Ohio had become too much for her, and she didn't want to admit it. All this was conjecture on my part, but it seemed to make sense. She had made that trip many times over the past twenty-two years and had never had a problem. Now, she was unsure of herself and scared.

The next morning, Lynn and I drove the two vehicles to the airport. I turned in the rental car and paid the extra money for the additional day. Lynn and I then walked Mother to the departure gate. She settled into one of the seats in the waiting area, and I approached the desk.

"Hi. My name is Diane Adams. My mother, Ethel, is leaving on the 9:00 a.m. flight to Tampa."

"Yes. I see her here. The note says she needs help boarding the plane?"

"Well, yes and no. She doesn't know that I asked for help, and I'm afraid she will get hateful with you if you tell her that."

"No problem, Ms. Adams. I'll just tell her it's a courtesy, and I will see her on the plane personally." Relieved, I thanked her profusely and returned to where Mom was sitting.

"What was that all about?"

"Oh, I was just checking on your flight, making sure it was on time and everything."

"Oh."

"So I need to get to work, and Lynn needs to get to school. Are you sure you're going to be okay?"

"I'm going to be fine. My friend, Val, is picking me up at the airport in Tampa."

"Good. Well, I love you. I'll be in touch soon to discuss plans to move you to Ohio. You be careful. Call me when you get home. You can just leave a message on the machine."

"Bye, Grandma. I love you," said my daughter as she tried to hug her grandma goodbye.

Mother's only response was goodbye. As Lynn and I exited the airport, I felt about a hundred years old. Although I should have felt relieved that Mother was about to board a plane for Florida, I could not shake the foreboding feeling that my world was about to turn upside down.

PART II

SIX

In January, I called Mother to discuss the plan I thought would work for her moving back to Ohio. I would come to Florida in February for her birthday, just for a long weekend. During my visit, I would find a realtor and put her home on the market. Once the mobile home was sold, I would come back to Florida to pack her up and move her to Ohio. By only taking a couple of days off for the first trip, I would have more time to spend on the second trip. I had discussed the plan with my sister prior to calling Mom, and she agreed with me.

"So I will fly in Wednesday evening. That will give me two business days to find a realtor, have the place appraised, and get a 'For Sale' sign in the yard."

"Do you want me to pick you up at the airport?"

Panicked, I said, "No. I want to rent a car. It will be late when I get in, and I don't want you driving that far at night. I'm scheduled to land at 7:05 p.m. By the time I pick up the rental and get on the road, I figure I should be at your house no later than nine."

"Okay."

"I did some research online and have numbers for a couple of realtors to call when I get there. Would any of your friends happen to know any realtors for mobile homes?"

"I don't know. I doubt it."

"Would you mind at least asking some of them? I really would prefer if we could get a recommendation from someone."

"I'll try."

"Okay. Well, I guess I'll see you February 7. Love you."

"Love you."

As I hung up the phone, I was fairly certain that Mother would do no homework prior to my arriving in Florida. She wasn't going to talk to anyone about possible realtors. I was on my own. It would surely be a nice surprise if I arrived to find a different story. But then, surprises are generally overrated.

Armed with my list of realtors, my overnight bag, and my plane ticket, I left my office and headed for the airport. I had said my goodbyes to the kids when I dropped them off at school. Hopefully, they wouldn't burn down the house before I got home. They were certainly old enough to stay home four days by themselves. However, they often quarreled more when it was just the two of them at home. I couldn't worry about that now. Their dad was going to check in on them, and Ben said he would drop by too. My focus now had to be Mom and Florida. I felt good about my approach and felt certain that God was the master of this plan.

To further demonstrate that God was in control, my plane landed in Tampa a little ahead of schedule. There was no line at the rental car counter, and I was able to get on the road to Mother's by 7:30 p.m. Southbound I-75 was practically vacant, and I made good time, pulling into Mother's driveway about eight thirty.

Surprisingly, she came out the door to greet me. "You made good time."

"I really did. It's good to see you."

"Good to see you too. Is that all of your luggage?"

As I pulled my bag out of the back seat, I commented, "I'm only going to be here four days. Besides, this way I don't have to check a bag at the airport. It saves time."

"I guess. I always check a bag."

"I know, but you always overpack too," I said, smiling. She agreed with me on that point, another good surprise. Maybe this trip wasn't going to be so bad after all.

The next morning, I was up before Mother. She wasn't much of an early riser. I took a cup of coffee out to the carport and sat in her porch swing enjoying the warm Florida breeze and talking with God. It was nice to have some alone time. Mom surfaced around nine.

"Good morning and happy birthday!"

"Oh, that's right. Thanks. What time did you get up?"

"Oh, I've been up since about seven, but I've been awake since six. Still on work time, I guess." We had a bit of breakfast, and I briefed her on the plans for the day.

"First, I am going to call the realtor and find out if she can meet with us today. I'm assuming you didn't find a realtor yet."

"Was I supposed to find a realtor?"

"I had asked you to ask some of your friends if they might know of someone."

"Oh."

"After that, we will head to the BMV to get your license renewed. I'm guessing you haven't done that either."

"Well, I figured you could take care of it when you got here. Saved me the trouble of doing it myself."

"Uh-huh." Two for two, I thought to myself. Nothing new here.

I called Sandy, the realtor, and explained what we wanted to do. Thankfully, she said she was able to meet us at 2:00 p.m. to appraise the home and draw up a contract. Efficient and organized—two things I liked best. Everything was falling into place.

This was where the wheels fell off.

I drove mother to the BMV where we waited our turn. Our number was called, and we approached the friendly worker at the computer. I handed her Mother's registration and indicated we needed to renew the tags for her car and for her mobile home. Both came due on a person's birthday in Florida. She happily typed into her computer then slowly turned in my direction.

"I will not be able to renew your mother's license."

"Excuse me?"

"Your mother does not have insurance on her vehicle. Under Florida law, the bureau cannot issue or renew a license without proper insurance coverage."

I turned to Mom. "You don't have car insurance?"

"Sure, I do."

The lady behind the computer interrupted, "Your car insurance lapsed for nonpayment in October of last year."

I stood there speechless for a few seconds while that sunk in. Clearing my throat, I asked, "If we get her insurance straightened out, will she be able to renew her license?"

"Absolutely. We are open until 4:00 p.m. today."

"Okay. Thank you."

As we turned to leave, Mother found her voice. "What happened?"

"Did you not hear what she said?"

"No."

"We can't get your license plates renewed because you have been driving without insurance since last October. What happened? How can you not have car insurance?"

"I don't know."

More than a little frustrated, I stepped out into the blazing sunshine with Mother following closely behind.

We got in the car and drove back to her place.

"If you got a bill from the insurance company, where would it be?"

"Well, there are papers on the kitchen table, and then I have a card table in the TV room with some papers on it."

First, I looked at the kitchen table. Obviously, she did not use this table for eating. I couldn't see the top of it for everything lying there. I found old newspapers, crossword puzzles, junk mail, and other assorted debris, but nothing that looked like bills. Next, I made my way to the TV room. The card table sat in the middle of the room mounded with paper. This was more than "some" papers.

Horrified, I pulled up a chair and started sorting through the mess. This was nothing close to what I had found on the kitchen table. Here, I found all the bills she had apparently ever gotten. Mixed in with the bills were cancellation notices. At some point, her cable had been turned off due to nonpayment. I found threatening notices from the electric and phone companies. I was too stunned to confront her, so I kept searching the mound for anything that looked like an insurance bill.

Lurking near the bottom of the pile, I found the elusive bill. Sure enough, it was due in October 2000. I also found several reminder notices threatening to cancel her insurance if she didn't pay. By December, the insurance company had given up on her and sent her the notice of cancellation. I took the bill to the kitchen and called the number listed. I explained who I was and what I needed. The person on the other end of the line was very cordial. She listened to my story, and then promptly told me that in order to reinstate Mother's insurance, it would cost us $1,500 for six months. The company would not insure her beyond six months at a time. I asked if it was possible to pay in monthly increments, but that was not an option.

"How about three months? Could we pay half of it now and the other half in three months?"

"Let me talk to my branch manager and see what I can do. What number can I call you back at?"

I gave her mom's phone number and hung up. My head was spinning. Even if they allowed us three months, where in the world was I going to find the money? I'm sure my face reflected my feelings, and I turned to Mom.

"What's wrong now?"

"Well, let's see. Where do I start? Because of your nonpayment and the fact that you never attempted to contact them, the insurance company is unwilling to insure you beyond six months. The cost for six months' worth of insurance will be $1,500."

"I don't have $1,500."

"I didn't figure you would have. I asked if we could maybe make two installments. She is checking with her manager and will call us back. While we wait, let's see if we can organize the mess on that card table."

As I sorted through the paper, I began making piles for each creditor. I had barely made a dent when the phone rang. Mother answered it and then handed me the receiver. The insurance company would work with us on payment of the premium. We could make two payments of $750—one today and one in three months. Relieved, I gave Mother the news.

"Where is your checkbook?"

"It should be on the card table."

"How do you ever find it when you need it?"

"For goodness's sake, all you have to do is move some papers."

Incredulous would be an understatement at this point. Instead of moving "some" papers, I moved some stacks of papers and finally found the checkbook. The last entry was fairly recent, and I was surprised to find she had about $1,000 in the account.

"Have you balanced your account recently?"

"Of course. I balance it every month."

"So you have a $1,000 in your account right now."

"Well, I just got my Social Security check and my pension payment, so that's probably about right."

I took the checkbook and Mother back to the car and back to the insurance company. Several years ago, Mother had added my sister and me to her checking account so we could write checks for her if the need arose. I decided I would pay the $750 for the insurance and then figure out how to pay the rest of her bills later. By now, it was noon, and we needed to meet the realtor at two. By God's grace, we were able to get her insurance bought and get her license renewed in order to be back home in time. Maybe after I met with the realtor, I'd go sit by the pool for a while. It had been a very stressful day.

SEVEN

Promptly at two, the doorbell rang. I opened it to find a pleasant middle-aged woman with dark hair and a winning smile. I introduced Mother and myself. We shook hands, and I offered her a cold beverage. She really didn't have much time to socialize because she had another appointment, so we sat down to business. She informed me of the process and asked to see the place. After a tour of the inside and out, she stated she thought we might be able to get $4,500 for the place. However, that was really the high end, and probably a more realistic amount would be $3,500. We were standing in the carport. I was thankful no bugs hit my tongue as my jaw hit the pavement. Recovering as quickly as I could, I commented on the low amount.

"Well, this is Florida. Do you know how many mobile homes are already on the market? Most of them are double-wides and sell for more money. With a single-wide, you just aren't going to get much out of it."

"I had no idea it would be so bad."

"I'm sorry. You can try another realtor if you want, but you are probably going to get the same answer."

"No. No, that's okay. Let's just go ahead and get a sign in the yard. We will take what we can get."

"Okay. I brought a contract along with me. We will list it for $4,500. The commission will be six percent. If we can get the $4,500, your net will be about $4,200. If we have to take less than the initial sales price, you would just subtract six percent from that amount."

My mouth was dry as I whispered okay and took the pen to sign the contract.

"Now, all I need is the title to the home so I can run the title search.

I turned to Mom, who had been oblivious during this entire conversation.

"Mom, do you know where your title is to the house?"

"It's got to be around here somewhere."

"Yes. Yes, it does. But do you know where?"

"I'll have to look for it."

Turning back to the realtor, she apologized for needing to leave for her next appointment.

"As soon as you find the title, just give me a call. I'll swing by and get it from you," she said as she handed me her business card.

"Okay. Thank you. I will start looking now and hope to call you by the end of the day."

"It was very nice meeting you, Ethel, Diane. I'll talk to you soon."

"It was nice meeting you too, Sandy. Thank you for all of your help." I just stood dumbfounded in the kitchen. God, help me. How am I supposed to find this title when Mother doesn't even know?

"I have a brown lockbox in my bedroom closet. It might be in there."

"Thank you, Jesus."

"What?"

"Nothing. I think that would be a great place to start."

Mother showed me the box on the top shelf of her closet. I had to stand on a chair to pull it down. Thoughts of her standing on a chair, falling, and laying helpless on the bedroom floor flashed across my mind.

"Hopefully, you don't have to get up here very often to get this box."

"Oh no. I can't remember the last time I had it down."

While this should have brought me comfort, it didn't. Given that she could hardly remember anything, for all I knew, she had just been up there yesterday!

I started sorting through the papers in the box. At some point, in her more lucid days, she had labeled dividers in the box, identifying the papers therein. I found a divider labeled "house" and held my breath while I looked in the slot. I did find a piece of paper there, but it was a memorandum of title, not an actual title.

"See? I told you I had it."

"Mom, this is not what we need. We need the actual title that you got from the state when you purchased your home. A memorandum of title usually indicates that the property is under a lien."

"Oh. That's right. The bank has the real title."

"What bank?"

"Bank of America."

"Why does the bank have your title? You don't still owe money on this place, do you?"

"No. The house is paid for. I borrowed some money to enclose the front porch and put a new roof on, and they have the title to cover the loan."

I needed to sit down. Back at the card table, I frantically searched for anything related to Bank of America. My heart sank to my stomach as I laid my hands on a rather thick payment book. I opened it to find several payment stubs missing. However, there were more stubs stretching into the future than had been paid in the past. I slumped in my chair as I realized we probably were not going to be able to sell the mobile home.

Gathering my senses, I phoned the bank to find the extent of the damage. I was put through to the loan department where an affable young man on the other end of the line informed that the amount of the original loan had been $11,000. While math is not my strong suit, it still only took me a nanosecond to figure out that selling the home for $4,500 was not going to alleviate the $11,000 debt in order to get a clear title. I thanked the man very kindly for his help and replaced the receiver. The word "probable" was obliterated from my vocabulary. There would be no more probabilities, only stark, cold truths.

My next phone call was to Sandy, the realtor. I explained to her what I had found and asked her to tear up the sales contract. We would not be selling Mother's home.

"I am going to run over to Publix and see if I can find a folder. I think I'll go through a drive-through. Would you like something to eat?"

"Sure. Can we go to Wendy's?"

"We are only going through the drive-through and bringing it back here. I have a lot of paperwork to get through, and I'm losing daylight."

"What are you in such a hurry for?"

"Because I only have one more business day before I go back to Ohio, and I have a mountain of work to do."

"Did you bring work with you?"

"No, Mother. It's not my work. I have a ton of your work to do. It looks like we boarded the Titanic and are headed for an iceberg."

"What are you talking about?"

"Never mind. Let's just get going."

I found an accordion folder in the office supply aisle at Publix that was perfect for what I wanted to do. Back at the house, I munched my food without tasting it as I plowed through the papers. I swept the entire card table clean and filed every paper. With notepad and calculator in front of me, I tried to brace myself for the bottom line. No amount of preparation could shield me from the results. All told, Mother was in debt for $48,000. Her monthly income was around $1,000. Even a CPA would have a difficult time trying to make these numbers jive.

I picked up my purse and car keys and headed for the door.

"I need to run an errand. I'll be back in about an hour."

"Where are you going now?"

"I just need to run an errand."

Once in the driver's seat, seat belt fastened, the tears just started rolling. I started driving, not even sure where I was going. I saw the clubhouse at the end of the street and headed in that direction. I found a parking spot out of the way and rolled down the windows, thankful for a bit of breeze. With cell phone in hand, I called my sister. Alaska was four hours behind, but I hoped I could catch her at home.

"Hi. It's your sister."

"Hello, sister! How is everything in Florida? Mom driving you crazy yet?"

It didn't take Carol long to discern, by my hesitation, that something was very wrong.

"Oh no. What's wrong? Are you okay? Is Mom okay?"

"Physically, we are both fine. However, I have uncovered a monumental disaster, and I just needed to talk to you."

Gathering what strength I could muster, I unraveled the thread of everything I had been through in one day. Stunned silence reached me all the way from Alaska.

"I don't even know what to do. At this point, she can't move to Ohio with all this debt hanging over her head. We can't sell the mobile home. I guess we could just abandon it, but then we would probably open ourselves to a lawsuit from the homeowner's association. The only thing I can think to do is call my boss in Ohio and talk it through with him."

"What can I say, Diane? I had no idea things were this bad down there. I had no clue Mother was in such trouble."

"Neither did I."

"I think your idea to talk to your boss is a good one. It's probably too late in Ohio to call now."

"Yeah. He's usually in the office past five, but I'm sure he's gone by now. I plan to get up early and call him first thing in the morning. As soon as I get a clearer idea of what to do, I will call you back. Will you be around tomorrow?"

"We will plan to stay home until we hear from you. Anything else can wait. We have to get this figured out."

"Okay. Thank you. I'll try not to call too early."

"You call whenever you need to," my brother-in-law, Pete, chimed in. "We can always take a nap later." We all chuckled and hung up.

I think I'll go get my swimsuit on and head to the pool, I thought to myself. I had promised myself some downtime, and I certainly needed it. An evening swim was better than nothing.

EIGHT

Needless to say, I did not sleep well Thursday night. Friday offered another brilliant day in the Sunshine State, but it did not offer any solace for the burden on my shoulders. The pressure intensely situated on me physically, mentally, and spiritually. By eight thirty, I had eaten a bit of breakfast and had a couple cups of coffee. I laced up my gym shoes and told Mom I was going for a walk. I knew she wouldn't want to come on a walk with me, but if I used the "errand" excuse again, she might want to tag along.

Once I was out of sight of Mother's place, I dialed the phone. My boss, Dave, answered after a couple of rings. Thankfully, he had no early appointments and had the time to talk. I laid out everything I had uncovered in Florida, and we discussed ways that would be feasible for me to move Mother back to Ohio. We ended up talking for an hour, but I had a firm plan in mind when we ended our call.

My next call would need to be to Alaska, but I wanted to try not to call before seven if I could help it. While I waited for the time to pass, I sat down with Mother to try to prepare her for what was coming.

"Mom, I called my boss this morning and discussed your situation with him."

"What situation? Why did you need to talk to a lawyer?"

"Okay. Here it is. You have no money. Your income is not enough to pay all of the bills you have. Because of the money you borrowed against your home, we cannot sell it. The bank essentially owns your home. I needed to talk to a lawyer because this is serious trouble. You want to move to Ohio, but only one path exists that makes sense for assuring we can move you. Are you with me so far?"

"I guess so."

"Please try to understand what I am saying. Stop me and ask for clarification if you need to, but you have to pay attention. This is critically important."

"Okay."

Taking a deep breath, I began outlining the plan. Mother had her estate-planning documents prepared years before, but we were going to need to revise them. The first step would be to prepare a new durable power of attorney, making me the attorney-in-fact to act in all matters on Mother's behalf. Her current power of attorney listed my sister as attorney-in-fact. My sister lived in Alaska, my mother currently lived in Florida, and I lived in Ohio. We had to consolidate the power in order to be effective. Dave was drawing up a new power of attorney as we spoke and was faxing it to me at the clubhouse. After we talked to Carol, Mom and I would go to the clubhouse, and the manager there would notarize Mom's signature and gather two more witnesses for us.

As Mom's attorney-in-fact, I was taking over all her finances. She seemed relieved by this idea. I told her not to pay any more bills, other than the utilities, to keep the lights on and provide her comfort until she moved. This thought perplexed her a bit, and I carried on with my explanation of the plan. "The reason you aren't going to pay any nonessential bills is that we are going to file for bankruptcy when you get to Ohio." She was shocked by this as I knew she would be. I explained that this was the only way to get her out of the hole she had dug for herself. If we filed for bankruptcy in Florida, we would have to hire a Florida attorney, and I did not know any attorneys in Florida. I knew many attorneys in Ohio, and I especially knew a bankruptcy lawyer. If we filed in Florida, it would mean I would have to make many more trips back and forth until the bankruptcy was final. I didn't have the money for that, and I was not about to enter the same black hole she was inhabiting. She only had to live in Ohio six months before we could file. During those six months, we would stockpile as much money as possible for her to start her new life and build the funds the attorney would require.

"I know that was a lot of information. Do you have any questions?"

"When do we sell the house?"

"Mom, we aren't selling the house. I just told you that we can't."

"Why can't we?"

Trying to remain calm, I explained the plan to her again.

"So we're just leaving the house?"

"Yes. We will pack your things and move them to Ohio and leave the house empty."

"Won't that make it harder to sell?"

My patience was eroding quickly. I did not know how to get the point through to her. I glanced at the clock and saw that it was eleven. It was time to call my sister. Apparently, she didn't get any more sleep than I got and was waiting by the phone. Since Mom had two phones, we could all be on the line together. I laid everything out to Carol exactly as I had told Mom. Mom had now heard the plan three times.

"Does anyone have any questions?"

"I think the plan sounds perfect. Diane, I can't believe everything you have accomplished in twenty-four hours. You must be exhausted."

"I'm a little tired. I didn't sleep very well last night."

"Neither did I. My mind just wouldn't turn off. Mom, do you understand what Diane is telling you? Do you have any questions?"

"I understand. When do I move to Ohio?"

Amazed at her response, I added, "Well, we have to work out all of those details next. I have to figure out when I can take two weeks' vacation. I'll need one week for the Florida leg of the journey and another week for the Ohio leg. I also have to find a place for you to live."

"Pete and I are on board too. We will fly to Florida and help you get her back to Ohio. We can arrange to come whenever you are ready, Diane."

"Well, that's all we can do for now. Carol and Pete, I'll be talking with you soon. I love you."

"Love you too. Be careful on the trip home. Love you, Mother."

"Love you."

As soon as that call ended, another call came in. It was Dave. He had the power of attorney finished and needed the fax number.

"C'mon, Mom. We need to ride up to the clubhouse."

"Why do we need to go to the clubhouse? The mail won't be in yet."

"We aren't going for the mail. We have to get the papers Dave is faxing to me. This is the new power of attorney I told you about. You need to sign it, and we need to have it notarized."

Begrudgingly, she got into the car. Seconds later, we were standing at the reception counter at the clubhouse. "Hi, Ethel."

"Hello."

"You must be Ethel's daughter."

"Hi. I'm Diane Adams. I spoke to you earlier about needing a notary and some witnesses."

"I remember. I'm Betty, by the way, and the notary, but I'll run over the pool and grab a couple of witnesses. Oh, here's your fax."

"Perfect. Would it be possible to make a few copies of it? I'd like to have at least three originals in case I ever need to give one to someone. I'm happy to pay for the copies."

"Nonsense. You go ahead and make your copies, and I'll get the witnesses."

While Betty was gone, I readied all the paperwork so the witnesses could get back to their sunbathing. When everyone returned, I explained what was happening and why we needed him or her to witness Mom's signature. The whole process took about ten minutes, but it removed about 10 pounds from around my neck. With the signed power of attorney, I felt a little calmer and a little more in control.

"Betty, thank you so much for your help. I can't tell you what this has meant to me."

"It was my pleasure. I'm glad I was able to help. Ethel, I hope we get to see you before you leave."

"It will probably be a couple of months before we can arrange the move, so she will be around for a little longer. Thanks again, and have a great rest of the day."

"Thank you."

I took the silent Ethel and left the office. She didn't say a word the entire way back to her house.

"Now that we have the business for the day accomplished, what would you like to do this afternoon? I might as well try to relax a little before I go home."

"It's too hot out here for me. I think I'll just find something on TV to watch."

"Well, I'm not going to sit inside watching TV. I think I'll go up to the pool for a little while. I brought a book with me, and it will be nice to get my mind on something else. How about when I get back we go out to dinner somewhere?"

"If that's what you want to do."

"Wouldn't you like to go to dinner?"

"I guess."

The pool area was empty when I arrived. Apparently, the locals only went to the pool in the early morning and evening hours. It was too hot for them during the day. I didn't mind. I had my pick of lounge chairs and put my beach towel down. Wading into the shallow end of the pool, I luxuriated in the coolness of the water. Does it get any better than this? After sufficiently cooled, I stretched out on my chair, opened my book, and promptly fell asleep.

NINE

For a while, life returned to normal back in Ohio. After multiple conversations with my sister and working with my boss's calendar, we settled on April 7 as the next trip to Florida. Carol and Pete were scheduled to arrive at Mom's on the sixth. I would get in early the next morning. This time, I decided to rent a pickup truck instead of a car. Hopefully, we would be cleaning some of Mom's clutter, and the truck might come in handy. I also booked a U-Haul truck for the move. When we were packed and ready, Carol and Pete would ride in the U-Haul, and I would drive Mom's car.

I was feeling good about everything and could see the path forward. Satan, on the other hand, had other ideas. Two weeks before my trip, I awoke to sunshine and cool breezes coming in my window on a Saturday morning. I went to the bedroom window to pull aside the curtains for better airflow. Looking out the window, I saw my car sitting in front of the garage instead of inside of it. Thinking this was odd, I went downstairs to investigate. My son had borrowed the car the night before, and I couldn't understand why he didn't put it in the garage.

Upon opening the front door, total understanding hit me in the face. The entire front of my car was demolished. Trying not to overact, I ran upstairs and into my son's room.

"Jimmy! Jimmy, get up."

"What? What's wrong?"

"What's wrong? You want to tell me what happened to my car?"

"Oh, that. I hit a deer on my way home last night. I barely got the car home, so I left it on the driveway."

Hitting a deer in Ohio is totally conceivable. Whenever someone leaves our house, our parting words are "Watch out for the deer!" I called my insurance agent to relay the news. Cathy, the one who answered the phone, took down the information and told me to have the car towed so an agent could estimate the cost of repair. She also told me I would initially have two weeks of rental car privileges. Hanging up with her, I immediately called the body shop just down the street. Within a half hour, the tow truck was there, and I went out to greet the driver.

"Good morning."

"Good morning. I understand you hit a deer last night."

"Well, I didn't hit the deer. My son had the accident."

"Okay. Let's get this vehicle out of the way for you. Does the car still run?"

"I think so, but I haven't tried to start it this morning."

I retrieved my spare set of keys and took them out to the driver. While it didn't sound good, the car did start for him, and he backed it away from the garage door. Now the damage was even more apparent. Silently, the driver pulled my car onto the back of his truck and returned to my front step.

"Ma'am, I'm not calling your son a liar or anything, but I have never seen that kind of damage caused by a deer. It looks more like the car collided with a brick wall or something."

"Really?"

"Yeah. I've towed my share of cars over the years, and I've never seen a deer strike look like this." Taking a gulp and feeling the anger rising, I thanked him for coming.

"Someone from the insurance company should be by early next week to assess the repair cost."

"Okay. What year is this car?"

"It's a 1992."

"Well, not to give you more bad news, but I don't think the insurance company is going to repair this car. It looks totaled to me. I could be wrong, but I think the repair cost will far exceed the worth of the vehicle. I'm sorry.

I hope I'm wrong."

"I hope you are too. I really can't afford a new car right now. But I do thank you for your honesty."

"You're welcome. Have a good day, if possible."

"Thanks. You too."

By now, the slow boil of anger had risen to fever pitch. I stormed up the stairs screaming at the top of my lungs.

"Jimmy! Get out here now."

"What?"

"Don't 'what' me. The tow truck just took my car. The truck driver said he didn't think the damage had been caused by a deer strike. He said it looked more like the car had hit a brick wall. DO NOT LIE TO ME. I want to know the truth. What happened last night?"

"Okay. I picked up Adam and Steve, and we went out the Will's house. We were horsing around on the back roads. Will was driving his dad's pickup truck. He sped up, and I was following him. The faster he went, the faster I went to keep up. Then he thought it would be funny to slam on the brakes. I didn't see it in time and crashed into the back of the truck."

Counting to ten, I then asked, "Was anyone injured?"

"No. Everyone is okay."

Given the assurance that there were no injuries, I kicked my rant into high gear. Profanity spewed from my mouth that would have made a sailor blush. My daughter emerged sleepily from her room.

"Mom! What is wrong with you? The whole neighborhood can hear you."

"I don't care!" I screamed back. "Your brother totaled my car last night. Then he lied to me about it. I then perpetuated the lie to the insurance company. Now I have to call them back, tell them what really happened, and hope I am not arrested for insurance fraud. I have every right to scream!"

By this time, I felt as if I had a vice around my chest. Shakily, I descended the stairs, poured myself a cup of coffee, and retreated to the patio. I needed to calm myself before I called the insurance company back. First, though, I needed to call Ben. I needed a ride to Enterprise to pick up the rental car. Ben listened to the story, occasionally interjecting his own vehemence, and said he could be there in about an hour. I then called the insurance company and reversed my statement. I guess the one bright spot about the entire incident was that it took my mind off Mother for a few hours.

TEN

A few days later, I received the news from the insurance company. The tow truck driver had been right. My car was valued at $2,500, and it was going to take much more than that to repair it. They proclaimed my car totaled and sent me a check. Now, I had a little over a week to buy a new car before I traveled to Florida to enter my next nightmare. I had learned long ago never to ask the question "what else is going to go wrong?"

Ben and I spent the following Saturday car shopping. We found one I could afford, negotiated the price down a little, and I signed the loan papers. While buying a new car should have been a happy occasion, I felt morose. I had to make room in my monthly budget for a car payment for a car I was not all that thrilled about. At least, I had transportation to get to work. The cost of my car insurance also increased, so I had to add that to the equation. The only way I could afford the insurance payment was to sign a waiver stating my son would never drive the new car.

Thankfully, the week leading up to my departure proceeded without any further speed bumps. I decided to drive my car to the airport and pay for parking rather than leaving it at home and risking my son driving it. My daughter had her own car by then, so she had transportation to get them to school while I was gone and get to her job.

I tried to relax on the flight to Tampa, but that didn't work too well for me. So rather than read or work a crossword, I turned to my Bible and prayer. At the time, I had no idea the miracles God had in store for me. In hindsight, I was so thankful I had spent that time in prayer. Landing in Tampa, I made my way to the rental counter. The attendant took me to the car lot to find the vehicle I had rented. There it was. A shiny blue Ford Ranger pickup truck. The bed even had a lid on it, like a trunk lid on a car.

Arriving at Mom's, my sister came out the back door and bear-hugged me. "I am so glad to see you. I couldn't take much more of her by myself."

"Uh-oh. What is she up to now?"

"Unbelievable! She hasn't lifted a finger since we got here. I thought I would get a jump on the packing. Pete went to the Publix store and brought back some boxes. I thought I'd start in the kitchen while I gave Mom the easy job of packing her suitcase for the trip to Ohio. I thought, surely, she could get that much done. Every time I went in the bedroom to see how she was coming along, she was just sitting on the bed staring into space!"

"Oh, great."

"I'm sorry. I shouldn't be unloading on you before you even have a chance to take a breath."

"It's okay. We don't have much time, and I knew I would have to hit the ground running."

We both went inside to find Mother making lunch for herself. I dropped my bag near the door and went to hug her.

"Hi."

"Oh, hi. When did you get here?"

"Just landed. How's the packing going."

"It's fine. Your sister has been out here banging around in the kitchen all morning."

"Well, we only have a few days to get everything packed up and ready to move. We've got to keep moving."

"I'm going to eat lunch. You, girls, go ahead and do whatever you're doing."

With this, she shuffled off to the front room and turned on the TV. My sister and I looked at each other. Carol's head looked about ready to explode. I took my suitcase to Mother's room. Carol and Pete were in the spare bedroom, and I would be sleeping on the couch. Returning to the kitchen, I began helping Carol unload cabinets. Quickly, we ran out of boxes. Pete wasn't able to get very many in Mom's car when he went to the store. Now that I had a truck, we decided to make another trip to see if we could find more. However, by this time of day, the boxes were all gone. The store manager told us a truck was coming that night, and there would be more boxes the next morning if we got there early.

With no more boxes for packing, Carol and I decided to go through the "pantry" and see what could be thrown out. The U-Haul I rented was not huge, but I figured it would be big enough for Mother's belongings if we could sort through things and only take the essentials. It seemed like a good idea at the time.

We got into the pantry to find boxes and cans that were appallingly outdated. This made our decision easy. Everything that did not have a current use-by date went into the trash. About this time, Mother walked into the kitchen, having finished her lunch.

"Why are you throwing all that food out?"

"Mom, we are only throwing out the food that has expired."

"What do you mean expired? It's in cans. It's still good."

"They put dates on cans for reasons, Mom. It's not healthy to eat expired products. You could make yourself really sick."

"I haven't gotten sick yet."

"Have you ever eaten any of this stuff?"

"No. I keep it there in case I have to evacuate. If a hurricane is coming and I have to go to a shelter, I can take my own food with me."

"So if the hurricane doesn't kill you, you'll let the expired food finish the job?"

"Smart aleck."

At this point, my sister and I could barely contain our giggles. We soon learned laughter was going to be the balm to get us through this. If we didn't laugh, we would be crying all the time. Laughter tears were much better than sorrowful tears. Having finished with the pantry and not having any boxes to continue packing, I suggested we all go to the pool for a bit. Mother and Pete declined, so Carol and I went by ourselves. Alone in the pool, we could catch up on everything that had happened so far. Carol and I never in our lives had trouble finding something to talk about. I listened to her frustrations and commiserated. In the pool, we etched out a schedule for the week. Returning to Mom's, we both felt more refreshed and ready to begin again. Thus, ended the first day.

ELEVEN

On Sunday, the three of us "kids" were up early and ready to go. Mother was determined to sleep in, so we opted to go see about the boxes. By God's grace, when we arrived at the store, we found a stack of boxes broken down and ready to go to the trash. We quickly started throwing the stash into the back of the truck. With them flattened out, we were able to fill the bed. Thanks to the lid on the bed, we didn't have to tie them down. We just closed the lid. Now, however, we were going to need packing tape to reassemble the boxes so we could use them. Inside the store, we found what we needed and picked up some bakery items for breakfast.

By the time we finished our breakfast, Mother was finally stirring. Carol had come up with a brilliant plan. Since Pete wasn't too keen on packing, she figured the two of us could do it faster. We sent Pete out to the carport with the packing tape. I backed the truck up to the carport so he could get to the boxes. He would be our box assembler while Carol and I filled the boxes. She also suggested we try to get Mother back in the bedroom to pack her suitcase. Because Carol had already been packing the kitchen and there wasn't really enough room there for two of us to be packing, I suggested I start packing Mother's room. My thought was maybe I could keep her to task if I was in there working too.

I began with her closet. Her suitcase lay open on the bed. I pulled things down off the top shelf where I had found the lockbox back in February. I decided the lockbox should ride with me on the trip, so I headed out the door to put it in the truck. When I got back to the bedroom, Mother was nowhere to be found.

I asked my sister, "Where did Mom go?"

"She has to be here somewhere. I didn't see her leave the house."

Probably because she went out the front door instead of the kitchen door, I quickly surmised. I finally found her outside walking around the yard.

"Mom? What are you doing?"

"I was checking the neighbor's orange tree to see if there were any oranges. Sometimes, I can get a couple, but it looks like they've all been picked."

"You take oranges from your neighbor's tree? Wouldn't that be stealing?"

"I'm not stealing. They told me I could pick them whenever I want."

Skeptically, I said, "Okay. Well, can you come back in the house now and work on your suitcase? You need to decide what clothes you want to keep out for the trip to Ohio. Everything else will be packed in the U-Haul."

"I guess."

Back inside, I continued with packing the things in the closet, and she continued to sit on the bed. Trying to ignore her, I slid the closet door to the other side, finding all manner of useless items. She had bags full of other bags shoved in there. She had a million wire coat hangers even though her clothes were stored on plastic hangers. There were three columns of shoeboxes. I started opening the shoeboxes, thinking she had papers stored there, but no, they were all shoes.

"Mom, do you really need to keep all of these shoes? Can we please donate some of them to Goodwill?"

"Let me see."

We started through the shoeboxes together. I was able to dwindle them down to two columns instead of three, asking myself when in the world she was ever going to wear any of these shoes again. I took the boxes she agreed to donate to the dining room. I decided to create a pile of things we could donate to Goodwill.

Unfortunately, since I had averted her attention from the suitcase, she was now going through the things in the closet. I changed tactics. I went through each item of clothing with her and made her decide whether it went on the U-Haul or in her suitcase. By the time we finished, we had a few items packed for the trip. While I was silently congratulating myself on this minor victory, Mother chimed up, "Let's go to the beach. I need a break."

I wanted to ask what she needed a break from. Was sitting on the bed too much work for her? Nevertheless, I held my tongue. I'd already been called a smart aleck once. No need to waken the beast.

I walked into the kitchen to see that my sister had all the cabinets emptied and packed. She had certainly made much more progress than I had made.

"Mom wants to go to the beach. Says she needs a break."

My sister looked at me as if I had three heads. "She needs a break from what?" she asked incredulously.

"I guess from all the packing. We did manage to get a layer of clothes into the bottom of her suitcase." At this, we both started laughing.

"What's so funny?" asked Mom, walking into the kitchen.

"Oh, nothing. We were just remembering something."

"Well, stop horsing around and let's get to the beach."

Carol looked at me helplessly as Mom went back into the bedroom.

"I think we should go to the beach," I told her. "I know Mom said she wanted to move back to Ohio, but now that it's happening, I think she is having a hard time."

As Carol and I walked on the beach, we talked over the last several months. It was time for us to label this for what it was—dementia. Neither of us believed that it was Alzheimer's disease. I had done research, and Mother did not fit all the criteria for Alzheimer's disease. She definitely fit the pattern of dementia. This wasn't just normal forgetfulness. Everyone, at one time or another, walks into a room and forgets why they are there. Dementia takes it to entirely new level.

We thought about how Mother wasn't paying her bills. How she couldn't remember how to get to certain places when driving. How she seemed depressed and sad. How she had been dragging her feet to pack. How she just walked through the rooms in her house seeming to be lost. We both agreed that Mom was feeling overwhelmed by the whole process. We left the beach that day with a new understanding and agreed to try to be more patient. This was going to be a monumental hurdle. Mother had a knack for hitting all the right buttons.

Another thing Carol and I discussed on the beach was help for getting all of Mother's stuff loaded onto the U-Haul. I had chronic back pain, so I knew I wouldn't be much help, and I was the youngest one. Carol and Pete, both in their seventies, had no business trying to lift furniture and boxes. Then Carol had a brilliant idea. When we got back to the house, Carol went to the phone book. She scanned the list of churches in the area and found a Lutheran Church close by. Carol and I were both Lutherans, and Lutherans tended to help each other whenever possible. No one would be there on Sunday afternoon, but we decided to call first thing Monday morning to see if we could get a lead on anyone who might be able to help.

Seeing the pile of items I'd collected for Goodwill, I decided to load them on the truck. Now to tackle the spare bedroom. This closet was much worse than Mom's closet. Carol and I stood in front of the open doors and groaned. Most of these things just looked useless to us. The walk on the beach apparently did better for clearing our brains than we thought.

"What if we just transfer some of this stuff out to the truck and close the lid? I'm sure most of this could be used by someone here in Florida, and we wouldn't have to move it 1,000 miles," whispered my sister.

"Brilliant. She won't let go of anything, and we don't have the room to move it all. That U-Haul truck isn't going to hold all of this," I agreed.

Silently, so as not to arouse any suspicion, we began sorting through the closet. We did have some open boxes on the bed, and we did put some things in them. Mother was watching TV and oblivious to what we were doing, so I quietly made multiple trips out to the truck. The items we thought worth keeping we moved to the dining room, which was quickly filling with boxes. With the truck full, I called the local Goodwill store to see if they were open. Thankfully, they were. The sooner I could unload this, the better. I asked Carol to keep Mom busy while I slipped out of the house. We managed to donate two truckloads of items before Mother caught us.

"What are you doing with this pile on the floor?" asked Mother.

"Well, we thought maybe we could donate those things to Goodwill," I answered.

"No! I want to keep those things."

"Mom, we are going to have to whittle some of this stuff down. We aren't going to have enough room in the U-Haul for everything."

"Well, then, we'll just put things in the trunk of the car."

"Your car isn't that big either."

"I'm sure there will be enough room to get these things in."

My sister threw up her hands, and I shrugged my shoulders. I couldn't see any way around this. We would continue to try to get rid of things, but I had a feeling she was going to watch us more closely from now on.

TWELVE

Monday morning, Carol called the Lutheran Church.
"Good morning!"

"Good morning," answered the church secretary.

"My name is Carol, and I'm from Petersburg, Alaska. I'm here in Florida with my sister helping my mother move."

"You sure are a long way from home."

"Don't I know it? The heat down here is about to kill me."

"Ha-ha. You should be here in July!"

"No thanks! Anyway, we were wondering if there might be some young men at your church who would be available and willing on Wednesday morning to help us load a U-Haul. We are willing to pay for the help."

"Well, I can't think of anyone off the top of my head. However, the Monday Morning Men's Breakfast is happening. Let me check with them, and I'll call you back."

Carol provided her with our phone number and hung up. She relayed the information, and we both went into prayer mode. We agreed to pack more boxes while we awaited the phone call. Both bedrooms were pretty wellpacked, so we began in the living room. The majority of the items in here were knickknacks. Mother loved useless trinkets. Using bubble wrap to make sure nothing got broken, we started clearing shelves.

"Are you dusting those before you pack them?" asked Mom.

Suddenly, I was transported back to 1970. I was helping Mom clean house because we were expecting guests. She had given me the job of dusting three deep shelves of figurines and collectibles. To me, this was a useless endeavor. The shelves were part of a built-in hutch in our living room, and there was furniture positioned in front of it. Who in the world would look at these things, let alone want to inspect them close enough to the see the dust? Mother assured me, though, that people were always curious about such things and someone would want to pick one up for a closer look. I rolled my eyes and proceeded to dust each item as well as the shelf beneath it. "Well, we didn't think of that," I said. "Why don't you dust them and Carol and I will pack them?"

"That sounds like a great plan," said my sister, a little too cheerfully.

Turning my back to Mother, I silently gloated. What goes around comes around. Just a little bit of payback. I chuckled.

In the midst of this mind-numbing task, the phone rang. It was the church calling back. Unfortunately, they couldn't come up with any names of people who could help us on Wednesday, but the church secretary had another thought. She told us there were moving services in the area that we could contact. Seniors were always moving in and out of Florida. She recommended one company that she had used before and provided the number. We called immediately. For $50 an hour, they would provide two men to load the U-Haul. We figured we would probably need four hours. Carol and Pete graciously offered to pay them, so I didn't have to figure out how Mother was going to afford it.

Gleefully, we returned to our packing. Things were really starting to come together. I looked around the room at the stacks of boxes lining the dining area and living room. We were making good progress, but I figured we still had another good day of packing in front of us. Pete had run out of boxes to tape together, and we were filling the last assembled box. Although it was close to noon, Pete and I decided to try the Publix store again. Unbelievably, the trash compactor was running late and hadn't picked up the disassembled boxes. We quickly threw them into the back of the truck. I marveled at the goodness of our God. His grace continued to provide for our every need.

For the rest of Monday and all-day Tuesday, the packing continued. We had more than enough boxes. Pete emptied out the shed for us. Other than her washer and dryer, the shed held her outdoor tools and paraphernalia.

By Tuesday evening, the place was bare except for the stacks of boxes. Mother sat down on the couch and started to cry. I sat down next to her.

"Are you okay?"

"I guess. Just sad."

"I know. You've been here for twenty-two years. Many memories. Do you think you can look at the bright side? You're going to be back with family again. We will be able to come visit. You can be with us for all the holidays. We will get to see much more of you without having to drive a thousand miles."

"I guess so."

As we all went to bed that night, I prayed hard again. If she was sad now, how was it going to be the next day when we drove away for the last time? I asked God to help us get her on the highway and headed north.

THIRTEEN

The movers we hired arrived exactly on time Wednesday morning. I thought if we could get loaded and on the road by at least 1:00 p.m., we might be able to get to the Georgia state line. Thankfully, it took less time than I expected, and we were ready to roll by 11:00 a.m. We paid the movers. Pete climbed into the cab of the U-Haul, and I got behind the wheel of the truck. Since Mother wouldn't let Carol drive her car, she climbed in next to Pete.

I started down the street with Mother directly behind me and Pete bringing up the rear. I checked my rearview mirror to see if Mom was okay. I thought for sure she would be taking a last look at her house, but she wasn't. Her hands gripped the wheel, and she was looking straight ahead. I'm thinking that must have been a God thing.

As we merged onto the Interstate, Mom was still following close behind. Traffic on the highway was more congested than I'd hoped. At times, other cars got between us, and I lost sight of Mother from time to time. I was very glad Pete was behind her and could keep a better eye on her than I could. The exit for the Tampa airport was a little tricky as we had to move quickly from lane to lane to get to the rental lot. I pulled the truck up to the line and got out. Mother pulled in right behind me. The paperwork only took a few minutes, and I walked back to Mother's car. She was already in the passenger seat, and she looked a little pale to me.

"Are you feeling okay? You look a little pale."

"I'm okay. The traffic sure was heavy, wasn't it?"

"I guess so, but I'm used to driving in traffic."

The U-Haul, with Carol and Pete, was waiting at the edge of the lot, and I pulled over to meet them.

"How did she do?" asked Pete.

"She seems to be a little shaken. I bet she wishes now she had let Carol drive her car. Are you, guys, hungry?

Do you want to get some lunch before we get on the road?"

"That might be a good idea," said my sister. "It might help Mother to calm down a little."

Pete said, "We'll let you lead. You can stop anywhere you want for food. It doesn't matter to us. We'll be right behind you."

So the trip north began. I had purchased walkie-talkies in Ohio. This allowed me to communicate with the U-Haul. I had a cell phone, but Carol and Pete didn't. In this way, we knew when it was time for a bathroom break, to eat, or just stretch our legs. Mother was quiet, and, frankly, I was grateful. The quiet gave me a chance to settle into the monotony of the road and think my own thoughts.

Around three, we left Florida behind and crossed into Georgia.

"Say goodbye to Florida, everyone," I said into the walkie-talkie. I sneaked a look at Mother to see how she was handling that, but she was just contentedly looking out the window. I don't know if she didn't hear me or if she didn't care. I hadn't gotten the hang of reading her yet.

"I think we should be able to get to Valdosta by five. This would be a good place to stop for the night."

"I think you're right. We are a little tired back here."

"So am I. It has been an eventful day." Turning to Mom, I asked if that was okay with her.

"Whatever you want to do. You're in charge."

She didn't appear to be saying that with any malice, but I still was unsure of her mood.

We pulled into a Holiday Inn Express just off the Interstate at 4:45 p.m. I felt we had made good progress for our first day. Carol and I went into the lobby to register for rooms. I would share a room with Mom. Grabbing a luggage cart from near the front desk, I rolled it out to get our bags. None of us felt like carrying anything heavier than our bodies.

After a nice meal in the dining room, we all retreated to our rooms to rest and relax. I gave Mom the TV remote, knowing she would want to watch something. I opened my book and retreated into its pages. By 9:00 p.m., I struggled to keep my eyes open and noticed that Mother had already fallen asleep. I closed my book, turned off the TV and the lights. I was able to get at least one prayer said before drifting off. "Thank you, Lord, for getting us through the first day of travel. I pray tomorrow goes as smoothly."

By 7:00 a.m., I was awake. A shower seemed in order, and Mom awoke as I was coming out of the bathroom. "Why are you up so early?"

"It's not that early. I'd like to get on the road by nine. My goal today is to get at least halfway through Tennessee. We need to make some good time."

"I don't know why you are in such a hurry. We've got plenty of time."

"No, we don't. We have a lot left to do once we get to Ohio. I only rented the U-Haul for a week. We still need to find you a place to live and get you moved in by next Wednesday."

Grumpily, Mother got out of bed and went into the bathroom. I sent up silent prayers. I hoped this wasn't an indication of how the day was going to go. The walkie-talkie came alive.

"Are you, guys, up?" asked my sister.

"We are up. I'm ready for breakfast. Just waiting on Mother."

"Okay. Well, stop next door and get us when you're ready."

"Will do."

I zipped up my suitcase, set it by the door, and checked the room for forgotten items while Mother dragged her feet getting ready. I really didn't want to set the mood for the day by being cross with her, so I sat on the bed anxiously waiting. A half hour later, she was finally ready. Knocking on Carol's room door, we gathered all the luggage and headed for the front desk. It would be easier to check out and get the vehicles packed before eating breakfast.

After a hearty breakfast, two cups of coffee, and a to-go coffee, we merged onto the Interstate. It was 9:10 a.m.; close enough, I guess. However, with all that coffee, I had to stop by ten thirty for a restroom break. Unfortunately, I would learn later that this set a bad precedent.

Inching up the highway, Mother was ready for lunch at noon. I rang up Carol.

"Mother is ready for lunch, but I don't really want to stop to eat. How would you, guys, feel about some fastfood we could eat in the car and keep moving?"

"We can handle that."

"I'll look for a McDonald's. How are you on gas?"

Pete chimed in, "We still have about half a tank, but it would probably be a good idea to go ahead and fill up."

"Okay. I'll find an exit where we can get everything done at once."

Because McDonald's restaurants are usually at every exit, it didn't take me long to find the perfect one. We pulled into a gas station and topped off both vehicles. Then we hit the restroom in McDonald's, ordered our food, and were back on the road within thirty minutes. Mother seemed content…for a while. Thankfully, her full stomach produced a food coma, and we continued without any other interruptions.

At 2:00 p.m., Mother declared she was finished for the day and told me I could start looking for a hotel.

Incredulously, I told her, "We are not stopping for the day at 2:00 p.m. We have many miles to get in today. I told you it would be a long day. We have to get to Chattanooga at least before we stop for the night." Pursing her lips and crossing her arms, she half-turned her body to stare out the passenger window. Unbelievable, I thought to myself. I used her silence to bring my temper under control. I didn't want to yell at her, but she sure could be exasperating! North of Atlanta, we stopped for some dinner and a walk around the parking lot. Mother didn't want to walk and sat in the car pouting while Carol, Pete, and I walked a few laps. It felt good stretching our legs and backs after spending so much time behind the wheel. We agreed we wouldn't be stopping again until Chattanooga. Crossing the Tennessee state line felt like a major conquest. By the time we stopped for the night, it was seven, and we fell into our beds exhausted.

Since it would only take us about six hours, with minimal stops, to get to my house, I decided we didn't have to get started quite as early the next day. We were in the home stretch now, and we were all eager to have this trip behind us. Still, we were on the road by 8:00 a.m. after a relaxing breakfast. I explained to Mom what the plan was for the day and that we would be sleeping at my house that night. This seemed to lift her spirits some and put her in a more cooperative mood. Praise God!

Travel was good that day. All of us managed a jovial mood, including Mother. By 1:30 p.m., the Ohio River rose on the horizon. What a glorious sight! In another hour, I would be home. I called the kids to let them know where we were and about what time we would be arriving. We pulled into my driveway at three and tumbled out of our vehicles. Stretching and laughing, we burst through the front door relieved the trip was over. However, my day wasn't over just yet. While the others collapsed in the living room, I got on the phone to arrange for showing Mother apartments the following day. I then called Ben.

"Welcome home! How was your trip?"

"I'll tell you all about it in person." I laughed. "I was wondering if you could possibly do a couple of things for me."

"Sure. What do you need?"

"I need to get my car from the airport, but I thought on the way we could drop off Carol and Pete at Pete's sister's house. They are going to stay with her for the rest of their time here."

"No problem. I'll be there in about a half hour." Now, I could sit down for a few minutes.

FOURTEEN

Much to the consternation of my mother, we left the house early to look at the two apartments I had in mind for her. The first was about two miles from my house in Lebanon. The second was about a half hour away. The pro for the one in Lebanon was that she would be nearby, and the close proximity would make it easy for me to take care of her. The con for the one in Lebanon was that she would be nearby and in close proximity. The pros for the second choice outweighed the cons as far as I was concerned. The apartment was brand-new. No one had ever lived in it before. It was about half the distance between my office and my home. The apartment was located in a senior-living community. Everyone in the complex was fifty-five years of age or older, so there wouldn't be any kids running around. They offered a clubhouse where she could meet other people and possibly engage in a game of euchre or work on a jigsaw puzzle. The manager of the complex also arranged for outings for the seniors where a bus would take them for the day to a park or historical site. My vote was for this apartment because I thought it most resembled the mobile home park that she left. Regardless, I vowed to give her two choices.

The first apartment was okay, but it seemed a little dark. It didn't have many windows to let in natural light. In addition, the carpet was dark and the cabinets in the kitchen were dark. It just seemed to me a little depressing. Thankfully, Mother said she really didn't like it much. This gave me hope that I could blow her away with the second choice.

We drove the thirty minutes to the senior-living community. I pointed out the location being West Carrollton, which would put her in a more central location where family and friends would have an easier time visiting. She seemed to like this idea. Score one for Diane! As we entered the complex, I pointed out the sidewalks where she could get some exercise. We pulled into the clubhouse parking lot, and the manager, Melanie, came out to greet us. I introduced her to Mother, and, for once, Mother actually acted congenially. Score two for Diane! Melanie indicated we could either walk or drive to the apartment. I opted for walking as I wanted to give Mother the impression that the clubhouse was not that far away from her when she wanted to participate in activities.

The apartment was located at the back of the complex. While the view was not terrific, looking over the local E-Check facility, at least it did not have any other apartments to look at or the parking lot. E-Check was the state's air-quality control check where people had their cars inspected prior to renewing or getting their license plates. If nothing else, maybe it would provide some entertainment for her. Who knew!

Inside, the apartment was beautiful. The living room had a large front window letting in light. Since the apartment faced north, she wouldn't get direct sunlight, which meant that her apartment wouldn't heat up in the summer sun. Other amenities were a dishwasher, a pantry, and washer/dryer hookup all in the kitchen. She would have two bedrooms—one for her and one for all the junk we had to move from Florida. There was a linen closet in the hallway. So far, she loved everything (love may be a strong word here). Then we got to the bathroom.

"There's no bathtub. How am I supposed to take a bath?"

Melanie chimed in, "This is a senior community, and everything has to be ADA compliant."

"What does that mean?"

Melanie looked at me questioningly and said, "The ADA (American Disabilities Act) requires all of our apartments meet all disability standards."

"I'm not disabled."

"No." Laughed Melanie. "But if you were to fall or have surgery and needed to be in a wheelchair for a short time, you could still live in your home and have access to all of your own things."

"What does that have to do with a bathtub? Old people aren't allowed to take baths?"

"Bathtubs present a fall risk. For some people, it's hard for them to lift their legs high enough to get into and out of a tub. There is also the risk of slipping while either getting into or out of the tub. For this reason, all of our apartments are equipped with showers where the resident just walks in."

"I don't like showers."

"Mother, we could get you a bench to sit on in the shower. Melanie, would it be possible to get a removable shower wand instead of the fixed shower head?"

"Absolutely," said Melanie.

"There you go! Problem solved. The shower wand and the stool would give you sort of a bathtub feel."

"I don't like it, but I guess I'll figure out something."

"What do you think of the rest of the apartment? Do you like it?"

"It's okay. Can I have a porch swing?"

"There isn't much room on the porch. What do you think, Melanie?"

"If you can figure out a way to do it, I have no problem with it," said Melanie.

"So, Mom, can we go sign the lease?"

"Okay."

We all walked the short distance back to the clubhouse, and Melanie provided all the papers that would need to be signed. I explained that I was Mother's attorney-in-fact and I would be signing on her behalf. Melanie was not sure if this would work but said she would check on it. The agreement also required that Mother be a resident of Ohio. Because this was a low-income housing development under Section 42 of the Ohio statute, this requirement could not be waived. I described how Mother had just arrived from Florida where she had been living for the past twenty-two years. I also mentioned that my boss was fluent in Section 42 and might be able to offer a way around this roadblock. Melanie said she would check with the owners to see if my signing the lease would be any problem, and I said I would check with my boss on the Ohio residency requirement.

Since it was Saturday, though, there wasn't anything either of us could do until Monday. I tried to remain optimistic. God had brought us this far. I was sure he wasn't going to let us down now. On the ride home, I enthusiastically covered all the positive things about the apartment, trying to muster some enthusiasm on Mother's part. I don't really think the word "enthusiasm" was part of my mother's vocabulary. I was just going to have to settle for quiet stoicism.

Back home, I called my sister to give her the update. While I was talking with her, I had an idea about the residency issue. Before we ended our call, I invited her and Pete, along with Pete's sister and brother-in-law, to dinner on Sunday. I thought we needed some enjoyment in our life at the moment. She covered the phone mouthpiece to ask her sister-in-law and returned with an affirmative vote. She also indicated she and Pete would like to attend church with us in the morning. Sunday looked to be a promising day.

Once I hung up with Carol, I called Melanie at Creekside to tell her about my idea. I wondered if an affidavit could satisfy the residency requirement. Unfortunately, she had already left the office, and I would have to wait until Monday. However, I decided to go ahead and draft the affidavit. That way, if the answer were yes, I would have it ready to go.

FIFTEEN

Monday arrived on the heels of a most pleasant Sunday spent with family. Mother seemed to enjoy the dinner I had planned, and she even agreed to go to church with us since Carol and Pete were going as well. Promptly at 9:00 a.m., I phoned the Creekside office, and Melanie answered the phone. Relieved to hear her voice, I presented my idea about the affidavit. As she hadn't yet called the owners about my signing the lease on Mother's behalf, she would ask them both questions at the same time and call me back.

While we waited, I enticed Mother to sit with me on the patio. I poured two cups of coffee and put up the umbrella. She actually seemed to relax while enjoying my flower garden. We didn't talk much, which was perfect. I didn't want anything to destroy the zen atmosphere I was trying to create. The only interruption was the phone call from Creekside. I left Mother to commune with nature while I took the call inside.

By God's grace, Melanie had excellent news. The development owner said they could comply with both requests. She outlined the specifics of what needed to be included in the affidavit, and we arranged to meet at the clubhouse at 2:00 p.m. I immediately went to my computer and added the language to my already prepared affidavit. Now, I just needed to find a notary public to notarize my signature. As banks usually have a notary onsite, I called mine. Sure enough, they had a notary in the office. I quickly printed the affidavit, said goodbye to Mom, and headed for the bank. We were now ready for our 2:00 p.m. appointment.

After signing the lease and receiving the keys, we went to the apartment. I wanted to determine the amount of shelf liner paper we would need, and I knew Mother would want curtains at the windows despite having the mini blinds. It didn't look like we were going to have to do much cleaning before she moved in; maybe just vacuum the carpet. I called Carol to let her know the deal was done and we could schedule move-in day. We agreed on the next day. Carol would round up some able bodies to help unload the U-Haul. I also called the phone company to see when we could get a phone line established. Since there was already a phone line installed, all they had to do was turn it on. They would do that on Wednesday. All we had to do was plug in Mom's phone.

I wanted to get an early start the next morning, but Mom was her usual pokey self. We were meeting Carol and Pete at the apartment at nine. It was all I could do to get her out the door by eight thirty. However, by the time we reached the apartment, she seemed to perk up a little. I took that as a good sign. Carol, Pete, and the helpers were waiting for us in the parking lot. Pete had already moved the U-Haul into position at the beginning of the sidewalk. Because Mom's apartment was halfway down the row, there was no way to get the truck any closer. I went ahead, unlocked the door, and propped it open. Items were quickly and efficiently unloaded. It seemed to take much less time to unload than it took to load it in Florida. The bulk of the boxes went into the spare bedroom, and the furniture was dropped into its appropriate rooms. While the men continued to unload, Carol and I put Mom's bed together. Whenever you move, you want to make sure you have a bed to fall into at the end of the day. I had learned that over a lifetime of many moves.

The truck was empty, the helpers left, and I took the truck back to U-Haul while the others worked on placing the furniture and starting to unpack. When I returned, Carol already had the kitchen cabinets lined with paper, so I worked on the shelves in the linen closet. Unfortunately, Mother was as useless at unpacking as she had been at packing. She was content to sit in a chair and watch Carol, Pete, and I do all the work. Pete hooked up her washer and dryer, and Carol and I started on boxes. We decided we would get the important things unpacked and leave all the other junk for Mother to decide where to put it.

After a very long day, we said goodbye to Mother and headed our separate directions. I was so looking forward to sleeping in my own bed. Finally! We agreed that we would return the following day and work some more. It was very nice to spend a quiet evening with my kids and go to bed early. I wondered if now my life could return to some semblance of normalcy. Hey, a girl can always hope!

Everyone slept in the next day, so we didn't get to Mother's until midmorning. She even had a smile for us when we reached the front door. The first thing I did was check the phone to see if we had an active line yet. When I picked up the headset, I was disappointed to find it dead. The phone company hadn't given us a specific time, so I would just have to be patient. More boxes awaited us. Around noon, we sent Pete off to pick up some lunch while we continued to work. Shortly after, the phone rang. It was the phone company checking on the line. Mother now had communication to the outside world. I decided to take Mother to the grocery so she would have some food in the house. I also wanted to show her how close she was to the grocery store if she wanted to pick up anything else later. At the store, she acted as if we had landed on another planet. She had no idea what to buy. "Well, let's start with the basics. You will probably want coffee, right?"

"Yes."

"You have enough staples in your pantry from Florida, so let's get some meats, produce, and maybe some eggs. How does that sound?"

"Okay."

However, as we walked down the aisles, she got into the swing of things and started loading up the cart with the things she wanted. We had doughnuts, Little Debbie snack cakes, and a huge Hershey's chocolate bar.

"Don't you think we should get something green or perhaps some chicken?"

Unfortunately, I turned the cart down the wrong aisle, and we were in the frozen food section. She was distracted again.

"I like these frozen dinner things."

I looked at what she picked out and knew it would be loaded with fat and sodium. Nonetheless, I relented and bought a few of them. A few more steps, and she discovered the frozen desserts.

"I need ice cream. Oh, and these Marie Callender's pies sound good. I'll get one of those too."

Somehow, I made it to the meat counter. I picked out a package of chicken thighs and a pound of hamburger. "I want a steak too. That sounds good. I like T-bones."

So we got a steak too and headed for the checkout. I looked forlornly at the items moving down the conveyor belt. I wondered who had kidnapped my mother. Growing up, our groceries never looked like this. Back at the apartment, we unpacked the groceries. My sister looked at me questioningly with each bizarre item that was pulled from the bag. All I could do was shrug my shoulders.

By the time we left that day, all of Mother's necessities were unpacked and stowed. We were able to get Mother to fill her dressers with her clothes so they would be where she wanted them. The boxes in the spare room were stacked in the spare closet. There was now enough room for Pete to assemble the twin bed that was to go in that room. As we said goodbye, I felt good at the progress we had made.

Pete and Carol were scheduled to leave on Friday. We had one more day together. After attending to things at my own house for a change, I drove to West Carrollton to spend a few hours with Carol. I wanted Mom to get use to her new place, so I decided not to stop by. She needed to understand that I was not going to be there every day. After all the time we had spent together over the past two weeks, she needed to get used to being by herself again. Carol and I sat at her sister-in-law's kitchen table and reviewed everything that had transpired during this whirlwind trip. We marveled at all the doors God opened for us. Whenever we thought our backs were to the wall, God stepped in and showed us the way. He had truly been with us the entire trip, and I knew I was in good hands whatever the future might bring.

Carol, Pete, and I hugged in the driveway. I tried not to cry, but it was no use. I was going to miss them so much. Now, I was going to have to take care of Mother by myself. No more tag teaming with anyone. No one to relieve the pressure. At this moment, Alaska might have been on the other side of the moon. It felt too far away, and I was already beginning to feel alone. I knew my sister was only a phone call away, but sometimes, that is no comfort when you just need a hug or a shoulder. Wiping my eyes and trying to be brave, I backed out the driveway. I threw a wave over my shoulder and started for home.

PART III

SIXTEEN

Before leaving, Carol had written Mother a letter, outlining specifically everything that had transpired the past six months. She reiterated the fiasco at Thanksgiving. She detailed the steps I had taken to try to sell Mother's mobile home and listed the reasons we were unable to do so. She mentioned my contacting a lawyer and the need to file bankruptcy in Ohio. She included in the letter Mother's new address, my work phone, home phone, and cell phone. She explained to Mother that I would be paying all her bills and, therefore, keeping her checkbook. She told Mother to call me if she needed money for groceries or other necessities.

She ended her letter with "We love you and hope things will work together for your good. We can't do everything, but if we all work together, we can do a lot to help you and make it possible for you to have a normal life." She signed it, "Love, Carol and Pete." Although I wasn't entirely sure Mother would ever read this or understand it, I was grateful for the attempt. I kept the notebook with this letter open next to her phone, hoping she might review it from time to time.

I thought I was doing the right thing by keeping her life as close to what she had in Florida. I thought it might help her adapt to her new surroundings. While I do believe I was on the right track, Mother seemed to withdraw into the dementia a little deeper since the move. I was so naive.

It had been almost a week since I'd seen Mother, but I did call her a couple of times to check in. I went back to work. The kids went back to school after their spring break. I was giving Mom time to adjust to her new life. The phone rang on a Saturday morning.

"Hello?"

"When are we going to the grocery store? I need to get a few things."

"Good morning to you too."

"What?"

"Never mind. You mean you haven't gone to the grocery store?"

"No. I've been waiting on you."

"You have a car. I showed you where the grocery store is located. I thought you could go to the store on your own."

"Well, I don't know my way around yet. I thought you'd be taking me."

"Okay. Are you in desperate need, or could we go on Monday? I could stop by your place on my way home from work."

"That will be fine. What time will you get here?"

"I should be able to be there around five thirty."

"Okay. Bye."

At least I had bought myself a couple of days. I could have gone that day, but I did not want to give her the impression that I would be standing by the phone waiting to jump at her every request. I was trying to set a few boundaries early on. I thought it would be important to my sanity.

Monday evening, I was driving to Mom's house when I became intrigued by the car in front of me. It looked like Mom's car. No way, I thought. If she won't drive to the grocery store, she wouldn't be driving anywhere else. At the stoplight where I needed to turn, this car turned as well. I got a better look at the driver, and, sure enough, it was Mom. I recognized the hat she wore everywhere. I wondered where she had gone. I pulled into the parking lot behind her, parked my car, and walked over to hers. She exited the car and looked a little shaky. I inadvertently startled her when I approached.

"Hi."

"Oh, hi."

"Sorry. I didn't mean to scare you."

"That's okay. What are you doing here?"

"We're supposed to go grocery shopping, remember? I told you on the phone Saturday."

"Oh, yeah. My list is in the apartment."

As we walked down the walkway to her apartment, I asked, "So where did you go?"

"When?"

"Just now. You just got back from somewhere. You just pulled into the driveway."

"I drove to Franklin."

"To Franklin!" I blurted. "Why in the world did you go to Franklin? That's, like, 20 miles away."

"I was looking for Paul."

"Paul who?"

"Paul Cook, my ex-husband. I tried to find him in the phone book but couldn't. Then I remembered he lived in Franklin, so I took a drive."

"So you just started driving to Franklin to find this Paul guy without having an address for him?"

"Well, I used to know where he lived, but everything around here looks so different. It took me two hours to find my way back here."

Completely flabbergasted, I just stared at her. "You've been driving around for two hours?"

"Yes."

"Did you even have enough gas for that?"

"I guess. I got home, didn't I?"

"Do you know if Paul is even still alive?"

"Of course, he's alive!"

"When was the last time you saw him?"

"I don't know for sure. It's been a while."

With nothing left to say, we retrieved her grocery list and headed for the store. I decided to drive her car and put gas in it just in case she decided on another road trip. I don't know what she would have done had she run out of gas on her little adventure. This was scary stuff.

On my way home, I called Carol and relayed the story. By then, the scary had worn off, and the two of us had a good laugh. I asked Carol if she knew Paul Cook's whereabouts, but she thought he was probably dead as I had surmised. Carol said she didn't think Mother had probably seen Paul since the early 1950s. I found that this is typical behavior for a person with dementia. They can't remember their address, but the memories from sixty years ago are as clear as day. I had so much to learn.

In thinking about the events of the day, I decided I would arrange with mother to take her to the grocery store once a week. I wasn't going to be able to go weeks (or months) without seeing her. Hopefully, she would connect with some of her friends from twenty-two years ago, if there were any left, and they might be able to get her out of the house occasionally. Until then, I was going to be her lifeline to the outside world. I decided I didn't want to visit the same day every week. I didn't want her to get used to counting on my being there on a specific day at a specific time in case I couldn't hold to that schedule one week. After all, I did have a life of my own. My daughter was finishing her second year of college, and my son was nearing graduation from high school. Although they were somewhat self-sufficient, I was still the Mom and still responsible for them.

On Thursday evening, I called Mom to see if she would like to go out to dinner Friday evening after I got off work. I really didn't want to get in the habit of spending my weekends there. This didn't mean that I would never see her on the weekends, but I felt I needed a little downtime of my own. If I was going to survive this dementia circus, I was going to have to take care of myself or end up the psych ward. She agreed to dinner on Friday.

When I got to her house that evening, she asked if we were going to the grocery store.

"We just went to the store on Monday."

"We did?"

"You don't remember?"

"No. I have my list right here."

"Okay. How about if we go to Wendy's and we can go to the grocery after dinner?"

"Okay. Can I get a Frosty?"

"Of course, as long as you have something to eat with it." I smiled.

I picked up the grocery list, and we headed for the door. There was one item on the list—ice cream.

"Is this all you need from the store?"

"Well, I might find some other things once we get there."

Now I understood. She equated my visits with going to the grocery. At Wendy's, we sat down to eat and to silence. This was going to be fun.

"So did you go anywhere this week?"

"No. I stayed home."

"Have you met any of your neighbors yet?"

"Why would I do that?"

"Well, I thought it would be nice if you made some new friends."

"I don't need any friends. I'm my own best company."

My eyes rolled up into my head at that comment. "What about some of your Eastern Star friends? Have you tried to contact any of them?"

"No."

Silence.

"Have you been over to the clubhouse to check it out?"

"No."

More silence.

"Has Uncle Ray called you? I called him and gave him your address and phone number so he could be in touch."

"No."

"Maybe you could call him. You have his phone number, right?"

"Yes."

"So give him a call. I'm sure he would like to see you."

"Maybe."

After the tortured dinner, we moved on to the grocery store. I got a cart and started for the frozen food section. After all, the only thing on her list was ice cream. However, Mother had other ideas.

"I want to go down this aisle."

Moving the cart in that direction, I asked, "What do you need down this aisle? It looks like it's just pet food, and you don't have a pet."

"I just want to look. All right?"

"Okay."

Slowly, we ambled down that aisle and then the next and then the next. It became clear that we were going to have to visit every aisle in the store. As we walked, she occasionally added something to the cart. Thirty minutes later, I turned the cart toward the checkout. We had come to the last aisle. Unfortunately, on our way to checkout, we had to pass the floral department. Now, we had to stop and look at every flower. Then she decided she'd like to have some flowers for her apartment. Thinking that might cheer her up a little, I acquiesced.

I helped her into her apartment and put away the groceries before heading home. It was almost nine, and I hadn't been home since 7:00 a.m. I was exhausted. While driving, I realized this was my life now. The sooner I accepted the situation, the better it would be for me. Rebellion arose in my chest, and the child in me screamed, "But I don't' want to do this!" Too bad. Time to be a grown-up.

SEVENTEEN

Spring turned to summer, and we had settled into a routine. Mother had been in Ohio for two months and seemed to be adjusting as much as she was capable. I learned to pick my battles so we wouldn't be arguing every single time I went to see her. Much to my dismay, I had ordered a subscription of the paper for her. Don't ask me why. The only things she read were the obituaries, the comics, and the store ads. The store ads caused me the most trouble. When I came to take her grocery shopping, she would have an ad lying on the kitchen table of something she wanted to buy. It was easy to say no to the most outlandish requests, but how could I say no to a couple of pairs of shorts on sale at JCPenney?

On one occasion, I found a newsletter on the table from the apartment complex. The manager did a nice job of informing the residents of upcoming activities, residents' birthdays, and a calendar of happenings at the clubhouse. I noticed they were chartering a bus to take a group on a one-day field trip and excitedly pointed it out to Mother.

"Look! They are going for a bus trip to the conservatory in Cincinnati. That would be fun. You love flowers.

I've been there myself. It's beautiful."

"Why would I want to do that? Be on a bus all day with people I don't know. I'm fine right here."

"But it would give you a chance to get out of the house a little. If you spent the day with these people, they wouldn't be strangers any more. You would have some new friends."

"I told you I don't need any new friends."

Right, I thought to myself, why make new friends when you've got Diane. So much for my idea of trying to make her life in Ohio resemble the one in Florida. She clearly was not going to make any attempt to improve her situation. "By the way, I need my prescriptions refilled. I'm about out of blood pressure medication."

"Where is your pill bottle?"

"I keep them up here in this cupboard."

Checking the bottle, there were three pills in the bottom. "Is this all you have?"

"Yes."

Frustrated, I looked at the label on the bottle. She had one refill left. I copied down the number to the pharmacy in Florida so I could call them the next day. Perhaps, I could have the prescription transferred to a pharmacy here.

The next day, I called the pharmacy at the Kroger store where I took her grocery shopping to see if they would accept the prescription from Florida. The pharmacist said that Mother would have to get a new prescription from a doctor in Ohio. They would not be able to fill an out-of-state prescription. I explained that she had two pills left and asked if there wasn't something they could do for us. The pharmacist asked me to bring in the pill bottle so she could see what it was. After work, I stopped at Mom's to get the bottle. Even though I had only seen her the day before and had taken her grocery shopping, she insisted on coming along. I explained to her that we were only going to see the pharmacist about getting her medication refilled.

After checking the prescription and taking pity on me (I gave her my most sorrowful look), the pharmacist agreed to give Mom a week's worth of pills, but that was all. I was going to have to find Mom a doctor and get her medication renewed. Elated, I took the pills and headed for the exit.

"Aren't we going to look around?"

"Mom! We were just here yesterday. Remember?"

"I don't know what you're mad about. I just want to look around a little."

Gritting my teeth, I put the prescription in my purse and asked her what she wanted to look at.

"Nothing in particular. Let's just browse."

I thought surely there must be steam escaping the top of my head. After twenty minutes, I'd had enough.

"Okay. We've wandered the whole store again. Can we go now?"

"I want to get some flowers."

"We just got you flowers when we were here yesterday."

"I want an African violet."

"You have three African violets already sitting in your window."

"But, see, they're on sale. If I buy one, I get one free."

Suddenly, it occurred to me. I was dealing with a child. We had switched roles. She was now the child, and I was the mother. We paid for the violets, and I took her home. Sullenly, I told her goodbye and slowly walked back to my car. I was so angry. All the way home, I railed at God.

"Lord, why are you punishing me like this? This is not fair! She is my mother. She is the one who is supposed to be responsible. She is supposed to be the parent. I have my own children to finish raising. Why are you doing this to me? I didn't ask for this."

The answer came back, "Honor thy father and thy mother."

Ashamed at making it all about me, I apologized to God and asked him for strength. I'd already been through so much in my life. I thought by this time I could be starting to think about things I'd like to be doing. I thought it was finally my turn to enjoy life a little without all the responsibility of caring for others. Instead, God's answer was, "Not yet. You will have that time in the future, but right now, I need you to do this." How could I disobey God? I certainly didn't want to. I had always tried to be a faithful servant. He had already asked so much of me. However, I was just going to have to suck it up and do it. He had always given me strength in the past. There was no need to start doubting him now. By the time I got home, I felt more peaceful but still apprehensive. Mother was eighty-two years old. She was in relatively good health, except for her brain. She could live another ten years. I pushed those thoughts to the back of my subconscious. It was too overwhelming to think about the future. I only had to think about today.

In thinking about today, I decided to call Uncle Ray to find out the name of his doctor. I felt a recommendation would be better than just picking a name out of the yellow pages. I explained to him how I needed to get her in to see a doctor as soon as possible to get her prescription renewed. He offered to call his daughter, who was a nurse in the doctor's office, to get an appointment. I suggested he get the appointment as late in the day as possible as I would have to take off work.

When Uncle Ray called back, he said Dr. Berks could see her the next day at 10:00 a.m. As my mind raced to think about the logistics, Uncle Ray said he and Charlotte could pick Mom up and take her to the doctor so I wouldn't have to miss work. I felt a whisper from God, "See, I told you I would take care of it for you." I whispered back, "Thank you, Jesus." Suddenly, I didn't feel so alone.

As it turned out, Uncle Ray and Aunt Charlotte both picked up Mom and took her to the doctor. While they were out, they took her to a restaurant for lunch and even stopped by the Kroger pharmacy to get Mother's prescription filled. When I heard about her day, I cried as relief washed over me. I phoned Uncle Ray and thanked him profusely. I told him what a relief it was not to have to take more time off work. He then uttered magical words that provided even more relief.

"Charlotte and I would be happy to take your mother to her doctor's appointments if that would help you out."

"Oh my gosh! That would be such a help. You have no idea."

"No problem. We're retired. We have the time."

"I'll give you gas money."

"No, you won't. You just save your money. Her next appointment is September 15 at 11:00 a.m., if you want to keep track."

"Of course. I'll put it on my calendar so I can reminder her. She won't remember. Again, I cannot thank you enough. This is the greatest gift ever."

Hanging up the phone, I was ecstatic. I had physical help. It was only once every three months but still. I felt lighter than air.

EIGHTEEN

By July, Mother had been in Ohio nearly three months. When I stopped by after work one evening to do her shopping, I noticed an odor, but I couldn't tell where it was coming from. I checked the refrigerator but didn't find anything that had gone bad. Next, I checked her pantry to make sure something hadn't rotted in there. However, inside the pantry, I couldn't smell the odor. Out in the dining area, I noticed it again. The light bulb went off as I realized the odor was Mother!

"Mom, have you taken a shower lately?"

"I don't take showers."

"So you haven't bathed since you've been here?" I asked incredulously.

"I bathe. I take a sponge bath in the bathroom sink a couple of times a week."

Trying not the gag, I asked, "What about your hair? Have you washed it at all?"

"I tried washing it about a month ago, but it's just too hard."

With complete astonishment, I asked, "Your hair hasn't been washed in a month?"

"I guess. Also, the perm has fallen out of it. When we go to the store, let's pick up a perm kit."

"You're going to perm your hair by yourself? If washing is too difficult, how do you propose to put a perm in?"

"I thought you could help me. We can do it this weekend when you're off work."

"Well, I'm glad I didn't have any plans this weekend."

I tried to look at the bright side of the situation. If I came up to give her a perm, I could clean her apartment while I was there. If she isn't cleaning herself, I could just about guess that she hadn't done any housecleaning since she moved in. I could make this work. After grocery shopping, as I was leaving, I told her I would be there at nine Saturday morning.

"That's a little early, isn't it?"

"Early? Really? I'd like to start early and not spend the entire day here. I have my own grocery shopping, cleaning, and laundry to do too."

"Oh, all right."

When I arrived on Saturday, she was still in her pajamas, but at least she was out of bed.

"I need to eat some breakfast and have my coffee."

"I guess you didn't set your alarm so you could get all of that done before I got here."

"I didn't need to set the alarm. I'm up, aren't I?"

"Okay. You get your breakfast and coffee. I'm going to start cleaning."

"Cleaning what?"

"Mother, have you done any housecleaning since you've lived here?"

"I do the dishes and pick up the living room."

"Have you vacuumed? Have you dusted? Have you cleaned the bathroom?"

"Well, I haven't done those things."

"That's what I thought. I'm going to clean the apartment while I'm here. I might as well do the laundry too."

"Whatever you want to do."

I screamed inside my head, No! This is not what I want to be doing on a beautiful Saturday, but this is what I have to do. Silently, I went into the bedroom, stripped the sheets off her bed, and started a load of laundry. She was still eating and enjoying her coffee, so I thought I'd start on the bathroom. By the time I finished, she was finished eating and had gotten herself dressed. I found a hose with a sprayer on it in her linen closet and attached that to the kitchen faucet. I thought this would probably be the easiest way to get her hair done. She could at least bend over the kitchen sink.

With the perm curlers in her hair and the first solution on her head, she had to wait twenty minutes before the next step. I moved the sheets to the dryer and started another load of laundry then began vacuuming all the carpet in the apartment. I rinsed her hair and put on the next solution for her to sit while I dusted all the surfaces. Finally, it was time to put regular curlers in her hair, and I could finish cleaning the kitchen. I couldn't believe I was able to accomplish all this before 1:00 p.m. As I was leaving, she even thanked me for everything I'd done. I was thankful as I drove home. This trip taught me that I was going to need to add cleaning Mom's house to my other duties.

NINETEEN

Near the end of July, I learned that I was going to have surgery, so I had to enlist the help of my daughter to take Mom to the grocery while I was recovering. I took Lynn with me to Mom's the week before my surgery so she could learn what to do and prepare herself for the frustration. I tried to explain to Mother that I wouldn't be coming for a couple of weeks until the doctor cleared me to drive again and that Lynn would be filling in for me. I don't think she grasped anything I was saying. The only thing on her mind was getting out and going to the store. I was so very thankful that my daughter was there to help. She got a big dose of Grandma and could better appreciate what I went through each week. I believe it was also good for Mom to understand that someone else could help her if I couldn't.

In early August, I was cleared to drive, but I would be off work until September. I surprised Mom by going to see her in the middle of the day on a weekday. I had gotten a notice from her insurance company that it was time to renew her car insurance. Our six months was up. Mother had not driven her car since the first trip to Franklin where she got lost and barely made it back to her apartment. I didn't want to pay $1,500 for another six months of insurance. She really didn't have the money, and we needed to save what she received from Social Security to cover the attorney fees for the bankruptcy that would be happening in the fall. On this visit, I explained to her that she needed to get her Ohio driver's license and license plates for her car so we could renew her insurance. I had stopped by the

Bureau of Motor Vehicles on my way to her house and picked up a book for her to study. She would have to take the written test as well as a driving test.

"I don't need to study. I've been driving all my life."

"I know, but I'm sure the laws have changed over the years. I don't think it's going to be as easy as you think."

"I'll be fine."

"Okay," I answered skeptically. "I'll pick you up Thursday morning. After the license bureau, I'll take you back to my place, and we'll have lunch before I bring you home unless you're in a hurry to get back."

"No hurry. That'll be fine."

On the appointed day, I drove mother to the BMV. The clerk did the little eye exam you have to take and handed Mother the paper test. She went over to a desk they had for examinations, and I sat off to the side while she wrote. I noticed it was taking her quite a while. For anyone who knew the answers, the test would have easily finished in fifteen minutes or so. She finally walked up to the counter with her test, and we waited as the clerk graded it.

"I'm sorry, Ethel, you did not pass. You only got a 60 percent, and you need at least 75 percent to get your license. You can retake the test again in fourteen days."

Frankly, I was surprised she got 60 percent. I thanked the woman and told her we would try again. Mother was visibly shaken as we left the bureau and drove to my house. She sat at the kitchen table while I prepared some lunch. She was very quiet as I sat down with her. Since the fateful trip to Franklin, I had been trying to figure out how to convince Mom that she probably shouldn't be driving any more. Knowing how stubborn my mother can be, I knew I would be in for a fight. Sitting at the kitchen table with her, I decided it was now or never.

"So do you think you want to study now so you'll be ready to take the test again in fourteen days?"

"I guess. Some of those questions were really hard."

"You know…you don't have to take the test again. You really don't need a license. I take you everywhere you want to go, and you haven't driven since April. The car has just been sitting in the parking lot. If you didn't get your license renewed, we could save quite a bit of money. When you think about it, we wouldn't have to pay the $1,500 for insurance, wouldn't have to buy gas and maintain the car, and we wouldn't have to pay the license fee every year. We could sell the car and save the money to give you a little cushion."

She sat silently for a few minutes before answering. "You're right. I don't think I want to take the test again."

"So it's okay for me to sell the car?"

She nodded agreement and opened her purse. "Here are the keys."

Jesus, Mary, and Joseph! I thanked them all. This was truly a miracle. I had heard from others the difficult time they had trying to get car keys away from parents who had no business being on the road. I lit up inside and out. If Mother had been paying attention, she would have asked why I was so happy. I excused myself from the table and went upstairs to my bedroom. I called Ben immediately to tell him about the car. We agreed that he would drive to my house immediately. We would both take Mother home. and he would drive her car back to my place. I just felt the sooner we got the car out of her parking lot, the better. I didn't want to give her time to change her mind. If she didn't see the car sitting there, I believed she wouldn't bring it up again, and she never did.

Later that evening, as Ben and I were discussing the day, it occurred to him that his brother-in-law, Bob, needed a new car. Bob had asked him to keep his eye out for something. This was perfect. He could buy Mom's car, and two problems would be solved at one time. After all the times God has provided for me in my life, I should not be surprised when I receive another gift. However, I am constantly in awe of God's grace and how he continues to take care of me. I did not deserve any of this. Thankfully, God doesn't judge whether I deserve his grace. He just freely showers it. I am so blessed.

TWENTY

My doctor cleared me to go back to work on September 11. I was glad to be getting back to some normalcy. As I walked from the parking garage to the office building, I marveled at the beautiful autumn day. The sky was cloudless cerulean, and a cool breeze rippled through my hair. I was pleasantly surprised to see that my desk was well-ordered by the temp who had been filling in for me. However, that pleasantness soon disappeared when my boss arrived and brought out all the work he had been "saving" for me while I was gone. What was the point of having a temp? Regardless, I logged into my computer and dove into the pile. About twenty minutes into my dictation, the other attorney I worked for stopped by my desk and said that a plane had just flown into one of the World Trade Center buildings. He was on his way to the conference room where there was a television. Others had also gathered and were watching the morning news. We all watched in horror as another plane flew into the second tower. Numb by what we had just witnessed, the realization slowly spread among the people in the room. Our country had just been attacked.

As the rest of the horrific news filtered into the office throughout the morning, I became quite anxious. I just wanted to gather my kids and bolt the door. By noon, not much work was being done in the office. My boss came out to my desk and told me I could go home if I needed to. I knew I wouldn't be much good to him the rest of the day. The shock engulfed me like a tightly wound cocoon. I had just been off work for six weeks, and now I was headed home again after a half day. My kids had both beat me home. As I walked through the door, I saw that they were just as shaken as

I was, and we attempted to comfort each other. As with most Americans that day, we were glued to the television set. In the late afternoon, I needed a break from the coverage and decided to take a walk. Even walking in my neighborhood was unsettling. The air was still and noiseless. No airplanes flew. Even the road by our house seemed devoid of cars. I cut my walk short and returned to the house.

Somehow, I was able to return to work the next day. All the parking garages were closed. The whole country was on edge, waiting to see if another attack happened. The parking garage was a block from the federal building. Most of the city was locked up. I had to find an open parking lot a few blocks away for my car. Although it was another beautiful autumn morning, I did not enjoy it as I had the morning before. In the office, we managed to get some work done which helped take our mind off what was happening in the world. After work, I decided I should stop by and see how Mom was doing. As I walked in the door, I asked her how she was doing.

"I'm fine, but I can't get any of my shows on TV. News is the only thing showing on every station. They keep showing those planes crashing into buildings."

"Mom, do you realize what has happened?"

"Yeah, somebody flew planes into buildings."

"Those buildings were in New York City."

"I know."

"Mom, our country has been attacked. Thousands of people have died."

"Yes, but why do they have to keep going over it again and again. I just want to watch my shows."

"Mom, do you remember Pearl Harbor?"

"Of course."

"This is practically the same thing. Do you remember what happened after Pearl Harbor?"

"Sure. We went to war."

"But didn't you feel sorrow for the people who died? Weren't you sad when Uncle Ray left for the war?"

"I guess. I don't remember."

"Do you remember how the country came together and sacrificed?"

"Oh, I remember that. That's when I got my job at Brown & Brockmeyer on the assembly line. My groceries were rationed. I couldn't even buy nylons. I had to take the bus to work because I couldn't get gas for my car. I couldn't do anything I wanted to do. Then to top it all off, I lost my job at the end of the war so some man could work."

"Well, I'm glad to know you were thinking of others besides yourself."

"What?"

"Never mind. I'm sure your TV shows will be back on in a couple of days. The twenty-four-hour news coverage won't last forever. Maybe in the meantime, you could work on your knitting or something."

"Well, I did take a walk today."

"You did what?" I asked incredulously.

"Since nothing was on TV, I decided to get out of the house."

"Where did you go?"

"I walked up the street but got confused when things didn't look the same once I turned around. That lady at the manager's office was leaving in her car, and she asked me if I was okay. I told her I couldn't find my apartment. She showed me where to turn, and I got back. The news was still on."

"I'm glad you made it back. That must have been a little frightening."

"I wasn't scared. I found my way back."

I thought to myself, And just how would you have made it back if it hadn't been for Lisa?

"Do you need anything from the grocery?"

"My Hershey bar is gone, so I could stand a trip to the store."

I often wonder how I could have been raised by this woman. We think nothing alike. I wonder where my compassion came from. I wonder how I've managed to survive my life so far. But I knew the answer. Carol. If it hadn't been for my sister, I would have grown up to be just like my mother. Carol's influence over my life, especially my childhood, saved me from the brink. She made my life bearable and livable, and I am forever grateful. Carol often says we learned how to live from negative example. If we hadn't grown up wanting to be the exact opposite of our mother, our lives would have been very different.

When I arrived home, I called my sister to share the bizarre visit with Mom. As we talked, my mind raced with all the thoughts of what could have happened to Mom if Lisa hadn't come along. Satan hit me with every dark thought possible. Carol and I discussed what we should do. Mother hadn't wandered off anywhere yet, but as the dementia became worse, that was a distinct possibility. We didn't think Mother was ready for a nursing home yet, but how were we going to corral her without making her afraid? She had enough mind left to go to the same dark places I had gone. I did not want her sitting in her apartment alone, thinking the worst.

After some research online, I came up with somewhat of a solution. I took Mom back to the BMV.

"What are we doing here? I thought I didn't have a car."

"You don't have a car. We aren't here to get a driver's license. We are here to get you a photo ID. It will have your current address on it and your name. It's just in case you get stranded somewhere and can't find your way home. Someone would be able to help you."

"Oh."

"It's just a precaution."

"Why would I get stranded?"

"Well, the other day you were confused when walking up the street. Lisa found you and pointed you toward home. Lisa won't always be available like that. So if someone else sees you struggling a little, they will be able to help you too."

"I guess."

"It will just give both of us some peace of mind."

TWENTY-ONE

As September turned to October, the time approached for us to begin Mother's bankruptcy. I contacted the lawyer and made an appointment for us. I had to take another day off work and just prayed I wouldn't get fired for all the time off. The year 2001 had not been a particularly good one for me, and I still had over two months to go! Mother and I met with the lawyer. He went over the paperwork with us and tried to explain the proceedings to Mother. She sat there with a hint of a smile, eyes glazed over, and nodding occasionally. I knew she did not understand a single word he said. He gave me a list of items he needed in order to fill out all the forms. I explained to him that I was Mother's attorney-in-fact and asked if I could do all this on her behalf. He told me I could certainly do all the paperwork and attend the hearings, but Mother would also have to be present at any hearing, and she would have to speak for herself. I figured we would cross that bridge when we came to it, but in the meantime, I wouldn't have to involve her in the paperwork. At least, this was a small reprieve.

When I got home from the lawyer's office after dropping Mom off at her apartment, I immediately went searching for the list of documents the lawyer would need. Thankfully, I had taken all of Mother's files and strongbox to keep at my house. Eventually, I found everything I needed. I called the attorney's office and arranged to drop off the paperwork on my lunch hour the next day. His office was only a few blocks from my office building. The bankruptcy petition was filed within a couple of days, and my prayers started in earnest. I knew we would have to attend a creditor's meeting with a court trustee and any of Mother's creditors who wanted to show up. I had no idea how I was going to convey this to Mother. I had to make her understand. The attorney had given me a list of questions that the trustee would ask Mother so I could better prepare her. This helped tremendously. I was able to coach her before the hearing.

The hearing was scheduled for 9:00 a.m., so I didn't have to take the entire day off work. I worked out an arrangement with my boss to make the time up by working extra hours. (Of course, he never had a problem with anyone working late!) We met our attorney in the hallway and entered the hearing room together. When it was our turn, the trustee addressed my mom. She was on her own here. I wouldn't be able to answer for her, and neither could her attorney. I was as nervous as a jackrabbit. My hands were knotted in my lap as silent prayers went to heaven. For once, Mother was on her best behavior. She appeared lucid and answered all the trustee's questions. He then had a couple of questions for me since I had signed all the paperwork. The entire event was over in about fifteen minutes. By the grace of God, Mother had done her part. Now, all we had to do was wait the requisite time for the creditors to object or file a claim, and all this would be behind us. Another hurdle cleared. I felt so relieved as we walked to the parking garage. Surprisingly (or maybe not), the only question Mother had for me was if I was going to take her to the grocery. Laughing, I told her no, that I needed to get back to work but that I would be back in a couple of days to take her to the store. In the present, she only had a one-track mind. In the past, however, her mind wandered in many directions.

On arriving at her apartment, a couple of days later, I walked into a furnace.

"Mom, why is it so hot in here?"

"It's not hot."

"It feels like 90 degrees. Let's turn down the thermostat and open some windows. We have to get it cooled down a little. You'll be comatose if we don't."

As I was opening the living room window, I noticed she had gotten her card table out and asked what she was working on.

"Nothing in particular. Just trying to stay busy, but all I can seem to do is cry." She started crying at this point and walked into her bedroom. She didn't come out until she had gotten herself under control. I asked her if she knew what was making her cry. She responded no and started crying again. My heart just broke. I knew a trip to the store would probably help and was able to get her into the car without much trouble.

After this trip, I made the determination to stop in to see her more than once a week. I knew she was lonely and depressed. I couldn't fix the depression, but maybe if she saw me a little more often, she wouldn't be so lonely. In my next email to the family, I asked each of them if they could maybe send Mom some mail each week.

"I don't know if it will help," I told them. "But hopefully it won't hurt. If she could get something in her mailbox once a week besides junk, it might help lift her spirits. She likes pictures, so maybe you could just stick a picture in a note card or something. It doesn't have to be a lot, just something simple. Believe me, I know how horribly she has treated everyone over the years, and I know she's paying the price for her actions. But if you can't do it for her, would you please do it for me? I just don't know what else to do for her. I wish this could be over for her, but for some reason, God doesn't seem willing to end her suffering. I fear that she has much more to suffer before it really is over, and my heart just aches for her."

Thankfully, my family was more than happy to assist. Mail began to trickle in for Mother. When I came to visit her, she would tell me who she had received mail from that week. One day, she had received a postcard from her granddaughter in Jackson, Wyoming, as well as a note from Carol. She so enjoyed receiving the notes and pictures. I really felt the mail was helping to lift her mood.

In November, I purchased two tickets for Mother and I to see White Christmas performed on stage at the La Comedia Dinner Theater. I thought this would be a fun outing for her. She loved the movie White Christmas as do I. I managed to get her to wear something other than her sweatpants and sweatshirt. The mood was festive as the maître d' showed us to our table. She thought dinner was delicious even though she hardly touched her food. She didn't pass up dessert though! The room became quiet as the lights went down and the curtain went up.

About fifteen minutes into the show, Mother exclaimed, "This isn't White Christmas!"

People around us tittered at her comment, and I just wanted to crawl under the table. Trying to hush her, I explained that it wouldn't be exactly like the movie because the play didn't last that long and they didn't have the resources for sets and props. She huffed, crossed her arms and her legs, and watched silently. I did see her smile at some of the familiar songs and crossed my fingers that she would behave herself through the rest of the play. When I dropped her off at home, she raved about everything and thanked me for taking her. I didn't hear again how it wasn't the same as the movie. I chalked it up as a success.

TWENTY-TWO

New Year's Eve 2001, I made sure to stay up until midnight just to make sure the year exited and didn't hang around for an encore. I began the New Year with hope and agitation. The events of 9/11 caused me to evaluate my life—where I had been and where I was going. Although I had accomplished much in my short forty-five years, what if that was the sum of my life? What if I didn't have another forty-five years? Were my accomplishments thus far enough to justify a life well-lived?

On New Year's Day 2002, I made a list of the goals I would like to accomplish before I died. I knew this sounded morbid, but I did not want to fail God or myself or my children or possible grandchildren. I wanted my life to mean something to those I left behind. Without a list, how was I supposed to keep on track?

One of the items on my list was a college degree. Although I had done pretty well for myself as a legal secretary/assistant, I was restless to do something else. Most people don't decide to start a new career at my age, but I could at least get my degree and check that off the list. I had seen a segment on 60 Minutes about a single working mom earning her degree online with the University of Phoenix. As the month of January progressed, I also saw ads on TV for the university. During a slow day at work, I decided to go to the university website and look around. The curriculum was daunting. I hadn't been in a classroom in almost thirty years. The business classes listed all called for statistics and economics. Math was not my forte. I didn't like it, and it didn't like me. We had an understanding. Eventually, my eyes fell upon the degree of information technology. My interest was definitely piqued. I had always been good at new technology and hungrily embraced new software whenever our office upgraded. Fellow secretaries were always coming to me with software questions. Another big positive was I would only have to take two algebra classes. Surely, I could survive that. (What I didn't understand at the time was that the six developer classes I had to take were akin to six more math classes.)

On January 21, I logged into my first class with the University of Phoenix. I was over the moon. Finally, I was going to get that college degree. Now, at this point, I'm sure you are probably thinking, Is this woman crazy? Doesn't she have enough on her plate already? And I would have to answer you that I did indeed have a lot on my plate. I was working forty hours a week, still had kids at home, taking care of my dementia-ridden, aging mother, and now taking on college as well. Over the course of the next four years, I would say to myself occasionally, "What was I thinking?" Unbelievably, though, I seem to work better under pressure. I often call myself a procrastinator, but I always finish the job and on time. Besides, this was a dream. I had to do this. The beauty of attending school online was I could do my work any time of the day as long as I turned in my assignments by the deadline. I was still available for my kids and my mom. I also had a week off between classes when I could catch my breath.

As the days passed, all of us fell into a routine. Mother seemed to be as content as she ever would be in her apartment. Each week when I visited, she would have a new story to tell me. Anyone on the outside looking in would think she was just a normal person with an exciting life. Those of us on the inside, however, knew the real story.

Mother was obsessed with the building behind her apartment complex, which she could watch from her living-room window. The building housed our state's "E-Check," an emissions checkpoint for all vehicles. In order to renew your license plates each year, you had to have your car's emissions checked. The only thing going on in that facility was cars coming and going. Not for Mother. The E-Check building was full of fascinating activity. I would hear these fantastical stories whenever I stopped in to see

Mom. For instance, one evening after work, I made my usual visit with her to the grocery store. Walking to the car, she says to me, "I saw Paul today."

"Paul who?"

"Paul Cook."

You may remember from earlier in this story that this was the dead ex-husband she has fixated on. "Did you go somewhere today?" I asked.

"No. He's working over at the E-Check now."

"Really?"

"Yeah. He has a food truck over there."

"A food truck?"

"You've heard of food trucks, haven't you?"

"Of course. But why would he have a food truck at the E-Check?"

"Well, the workers there have to eat, don't they?"

"Sure. So did you talk to him?"

"Oh no. He was too busy for that. I just sat and watched him work."

On other occasions, Paul was a mechanic that worked over there. For some reason, she tied Paul to that building. I still have no idea why. The fantasy life she had built around him emanated from that spot. I guess maybe it had less to do with the building and more to do with the comfortable spot in her mind where Paul lived. This was her way of verbalizing her thoughts. Would a psychologist consider this delusional? Perhaps. However, in Mother's mind, all this made perfect sense. In her mind, she and Paul had a storybook romance. In talking to my sister, I knew that wasn't true, and I still couldn't figure out why Paul was so important to her. I think maybe she sensed somewhere deep in her being that she was struggling. I believe she was scared deep down because she just couldn't think straight. Keeping Paul in her mind helped her return to a time in her life when she felt happy and secure. She needed to hang onto something that was familiar.

Repeatedly, Mother would ask when she was going to be able to go home. No matter how often I told her she was home, her thoughts turned to Florida. Once again, I reminded her that moving to Ohio was her idea. I asked her if she remembered wanting to leave Florida. I would refer her to the notebook Carol had left her, but she didn't want to read that. She didn't want to hear that any of this was her idea.

One day, out of the blue, she turned to me in hostility. "What did you do with my porch swing? Did you leave that in Florida?"

"Mom, remember, we brought your porch swing. You had it here for a while until that storm came last month and tore it all up."

"Well, why haven't you gotten me a new one? I want a new swing so I can sit outside."

"So far, I haven't been able to find one. This late in the season, all the stores are sold out of them."

"It's not late in the season. It's only June."

"I understand, but people generally buy outdoor furniture in April or May. Stores don't restock that sort of thing later in the summer because they don't want to be stuck with it."

"Surely, someone has a porch swing."

Frustrated with trying to reason with her, I told her I would scour the earth until I found one. If I had known about Amazon back then, all my problems would have been solved. Instead, I traveled from store to store looking for a new porch swing. My sanity depended upon finding it. One evening returning home from taking Mother to the grocery, I happened to glance at the parking lot of a Home Depot store. There was a huge white tent set up with all sorts of items on display. I turned the car around and pulled into the parking lot. Sure enough, they were having a clearance sale on all their outdoor furniture. The heavens opened, and the angels descended on a swing just sitting there waiting for me. Praise God! I spoke with the salesperson staffing the tent. This swing was the only one they had left.

"Would you be willing to hold it for me until I can get a truck here to pick it up?" I asked.

The salesperson hesitated. "I don't know. I'll have to ask my boss. We really want to get rid of everything. If I hold it for you, I could miss selling it to someone else."

"How about if I pay for it now and pick it up tomorrow?"

"We're really trying to get this area cleaned out. I don't know if my boss will go for that."

"Please. I'm desperate."

"Let's go inside and see what my boss says."

I followed her into the building. After some more pleading, I was finally successful in completing the sale. I practically ran to the register to pay for it, and they put a "sold" sign on it. Once in the car, I called Ben to find out if we could pick it up the next evening and deliver it to Mom. He agreed.

The next evening, we delivered the swing to Mom. We set it up for her, and, for once, she had a smile on her face. She sat down, and for a few days, at least, there was peace in my universe.

TWENTY-THREE

I sat in my office at work looking out the window. The day had dawned bright and balmy. The thought of Mom popped into my head. Call me crazy, but when this sort of thing happens to me, I take it as a sign from God. I decided to call Mom and see if I could get her to go outside on such a beautiful day. It would certainly do her good to blow some of the cobwebs out of her brain and enjoy the warm sunshine. I dialed her number and listened as her phone rang and rang and rang. After about twenty rings with no answer, I felt panic start in my stomach. Maybe I dialed the wrong number. I doubted it, but you never know. I tried again and got the same continual ring. Now the panic had risen from my stomach to my throat. I told my boss what was going on and that I needed to check on Mother. I would just use the time as my lunch hour. I made it to Mom's door in about ten minutes and rang the doorbell. If she didn't answer the doorbell, I was prepared to use my key. I was shocked when Mom answered the door.

"Oh, hi. Are you here to take me to the grocery?"

"Um, no. I came because I've been trying to reach you and you weren't answering your phone. I thought something was wrong."

"Nothing's wrong."

"Then why aren't you answering your phone? Did you hear it ring?"

"Of course, I heard it ring. I'm not deaf."

"But why didn't you answer it?" I questioned. By now, it wasn't panic rising in me, it was my blood pressure.

"Oh, that man down at the end of the walk keeps calling."

"What man?"

"That man that lives down there," she said as she pointed down the sidewalk.

"Do you know this man?"

"No. I just see him walking up and down the sidewalk."

"Then how do you know he's calling you?"

"Oh, it's him, all right. He calls and then doesn't say anything. He just sits there." Confused, I asked, "If he doesn't say anything, then how do you know it's him?"

"I just know! Okay!"

With my ire rising along with her belligerence, I knew we weren't going to get anywhere with this conversation.

"Okay. But, Mom, I need to be able to get in touch with you. I need you to answer your phone. I thought you had an answering machine. Where is it?"

"It's in the closet. I don't want that guy leaving messages on my answering machine. He's the only one who calls."

"Mom, that's not true. I call you. Carol calls you. I'm sure Uncle Ray calls you occasionally. We all have to be able to reach you. We need to plug the answering machine back in. If you aren't going to answer your phone, all of us need to have the ability to at least leave you a message so you know we need to talk to you. Show me where the machine is."

Mother took me to the hall closet. Sure enough, sitting on the shelf was the answering machine. I took it and plugged it back into her phone, set the time, and made sure there was an outgoing message on it. "Please leave this plugged in. Okay?"

"Okay."

"Thank you. I've got to get back to work now."

"You aren't going to take me to the store?"

"I left work to come check on you because I couldn't reach you by phone. I'm using my lunch-hour time for this trip. I can't take you to the store at this moment, but I'll stop by again after work and we can go then."

"All right."

"Have you been outside yet today? It is a beautiful day for sitting on your swing."

"It's too cold to sit on my swing."

"Mom, it isn't. The temperature is in the seventies. It's gorgeous out. Put a sweater on or something. You really shouldn't miss this. Get some fresh air. Clear out the cobwebs."

"What cobwebs?"

"In your brain! The bright day will put you in a good mood."

"There's nothing wrong with me."

My eyes rolled for the forty-seventh million time as I opened the door. "Of course, there isn't. Just thought you could do with some fresh air. I have to get back to work. I will see you this evening. Bye."

She said goodbye and closed the door. I knew she wasn't going to sit on her swing. I knew she wasn't going to do anything good for herself. Why do I even try? I try because maybe, just maybe, one time I'll get through.

TWENTY-FOUR

As promised, I went to Mother's after work. I really didn't want to go. I was tired, and I had already had one dose of her that day. Regardless, I promised whether she would remember or not. When I got there, she was sitting on her swing with her coat on.

"You decided to sit outside after all," I proclaimed.

"I've been sitting here waiting for you."

"For how long?"

"I don't know."

"Okay. Do you have your grocery list?"

She pulled her hand out of her pocket with a piece of paper. The paper contained two lines—Hershey bar and Krispy Kreme doughnuts.

"Not much of a list," I said.

"I don't need much."

"Well, I need to use the bathroom before we go, and I'll just have a look around to see if there is anything else we can pick up while at the store."

I opened her refrigerator, which was practically empty. At least, there was food in her freezer. While I was looking in the freezer, she piped up, "I forgot. I do need some ice cream."

"I notice you don't have any eggs or other protein."

"I don't eat many eggs. Too much cholesterol."

"An egg now and then is not going to hurt you, Mother."

I then turned my attention to her pill bottles sitting on the counter. I couldn't remember the last time we filled her prescriptions, so I looked at the bottles. The last time they were filled was March. The prescriptions were for ninety days, so I thought we should probably get those filled too. I was surprised and alarmed when I lifted the bottles and they were practically full.

"Mom, have you been taking your pills?"

"Of course. I take them every morning with my breakfast."

Not wanting to get into another endless stream of nonsense, I decided to count the pills. Each bottle contained about forty-five pills. There should have been less than ten by my calculation. How should I handle this?

She was just going to keep insisting that she's taking her medication when clearly she wasn't.

"Do you have one of those pill caddies that helps you remember to take your medication?"

"I used to have one of those. I don't know where it is now or if I even still have it. Carol probably threw it out."

"Okay. Carol hasn't even been here for almost a year. How could she have thrown out your pill container?"

"When the two of you moved me into this hellhole."

"Mom, I resent that. This is not a hellhole. This is a very nice apartment. It was brand-new when you moved in here. It had never even been lived in before."

"Whatever. Let's just go to the store and get it over with."

My thoughts exactly. The sooner the better. At the store, I tried to talk her into getting some actual food instead of sugar-laden by-products. I steered her toward the salad bar. "How about a salad this week?" She looked at the offerings and picked up a small container. I felt a small spark of joy. She managed to pick out some salad items that she liked.

"How about some chicken to go with your salad?"

"I'd really like to have a T-bone."

"You didn't want any eggs because of the cholesterol, but you want a big hunk of red meat?"

"Steak isn't that bad for you. I haven't had one in a while."

Glad to get some kind of protein into her, I reluctantly let her pick out a steak. Making our way through the store, we passed the deli.

"How about if we get you some lunch meat? You could make a sandwich."

"No. I don't think so, but that fried chicken looks good."

Of course, it does, I thought to myself. Well, I guess if she's going to clog her arteries anyway, it might as well be with fried stuff in addition to the sugar. As I thought about her food choices, I came to the realization that she really should be allowed to eat whatever she wanted. She was eighty-three years old. Why was I trying to make her eat healthy? In the grand scheme of things, she probably didn't have many years left. Why shouldn't she enjoy as much as she could in that time? I decided that I would stop obsessing over what she ate. I would continue to try to steer good food her way, but if she declined, I wasn't going to make a big deal out of it. We both needed a break from the drama.

When I got home, I created a note document on my phone. After all that had happened that day, I needed to pay better attention. I added to the note the number of pills I'd found in Mother's bottles with the date. When I went the following week, I would count again to see how many she had taken. I had bought her a new pill caddy at the grocery store and filled it before I left. I was praying this would help her keep better track of her medication.

I needed to call my sister to give her an update on Mother. About the only good thing of my sister's living in Alaska was the time zone. With her being four time zones behind me, I could call any time in the evening and she would still be up. I finished my homework, turned it in, and called her before I went to bed. My sister was always a good shoulder to cry on or ear to listen. She agreed with my decision to quit badgering Mother about the food she ate. She thought to idea of the pill caddy was a good one and approved my plan to count pills each week to see how often Mother was taking her medication. Hearing words of encouragement calmed me, and I was able to sleep after our call.

So many times, I wished my sister lived nearby. We hadn't lived near each other since I was nineteen years old, so you would think I would be used to it by now. However, struggling with Mom only made the distance worse. I knew she was only a phone call away, but that didn't help much when you just needed to see someone. During the times when I missed her the most, I would just hug my kids or have lunch with my best friend. I had plenty of people around me who would listen and give hugs. I just needed to stop feeling sorry for myself and move on.

TWENTY-FIVE

For the next several years, our lives orbited around Mother in much the same way. I included her in holiday celebrations whether she wanted to go or not. I was trying to provide interaction with other people instead of her time only being spent with me. Occasionally, my daughter would take her to the grocery for me, giving me a break for the week. Instead of continuing to perm her hair myself, I took her to the beauty salon. We went out to dinner or lunch together and to the mall for some new clothes I was trying so hard to make life as normal as possible. But there was nothing normal about this life.

Mother slipped farther and farther into her own mind. The dementia worsened along with the delusions and paranoia. Eventually, I gave into it. You cannot speak logic with an illogical person. I gave up trying to reason with her or correct her when she was outright wrong. To keep my stress level down, I sent weekly email reports to my sister and two of my nieces who were online—one in Wyoming, the other in Alaska with my sister. By writing down Mother's antics, I could turn them into humorous anecdotes. I also found that if I went along with Mother's craziness, I could turn her from that thinking and move her onto another topic. For instance, after hearing about the man at the end of the sidewalk calling her, I finally asked her if I should call the police. "If he is harassing you like this, maybe I should call the police."

"Oh, I don't think you need to do that," she acquiesced.

"But harassment is serious business. Should I at least let them know over at the office? Maybe they could go talk to him."

"No. I don't want him to get into trouble on my account."

Soon, there was no more talk of the man down the sidewalk. She was getting no more harassing phone calls, and she never saw him again.

The stories coming from the E-Check facility became more and more bizarre. Once, she told me a circus had set up over there in the yard.

"A circus?" I questioned. "With tents and animals and clowns?"

"Yep."

"Well, that must have been fun to watch."

"I couldn't see much when they went into the tents, but I got to watch them set up and tear down."

The circus didn't last long and was gone within a week. I asked her the following week where the circus had gone.

"They don't stay in one place very long. I'm sure they moved on to the next city, but it was fun having them here for a while."

How do you reason with that? You don't. You just have to go along with it. I knew there was no circus camped at the E-Check, but in Mother's mind it made perfect sense. What reason would there be for me to doubt her? From the time I moved Mom from Florida, I researched and read everything I could find about dementia. I had no personal references to lead me. I was flying by the seat of my pants.

I went through a time when I was angry with God for putting all this on me. Thank goodness, he has big shoulders because I unloaded a lot. However, through his grace, I began to settle down, listen to his voice, and look for his signs. God and I came to an understanding. More accurately put, I came to understand God better. My logical mind told me that God was not punishing me. He put me in this position because I was the best person for the job.

Carol was always available by phone, and we began talking and/or emailing at least once a week. We encouraged each other. Frankly, I think I received more encouragement from her than I gave in return. However, one day, she let me know that wasn't the case. She was dreading calling Mother, so she called me first. She told me how our conversations uplifted her, and she needed some uplifting before talking to Mom. Spending time with Mom, either on the phone or in person, was certainly a drain on the spirit. My sister offered some sage advice.

"I always pray first before I call Mother," she said. "God helps me get through the phone call, and he always helps me to know what to say."

Thereafter, I began putting my sister's advice to good use. I dreaded having to go to Mother's house every week. Many of you probably find my attitude detestable. However, as hard as I tried to put past hurts behind me, the scars were still there and still hurt occasionally. One word from my mother could send me straight back to my childhood. Why wouldn't I dread spending time with a person who could make me feel so worthless? My only defense became to pray first. It worked. I found that if I came before God before I came to my mother, our visits went so much better. God affirmed me as a person and gave me the courage and strength to combat whatever my mother may happen to throw my way. God knows the history between my mother and me. He knew exactly what both of us needed from the relationship, and, lovingly, he provided for both of us.

Eventually, I began to look at my past with Mother in a different light. Instead of looking at all the darkness, I decided to try to focus on the things from my past that brought some happy memories. Shifting my focus helped with the past and the present.

My mom had worked all her life. She was never a stay-at-home mom. I learned at a very young age to fend for myself. When I was seven years old, I was walking almost a mile to school. Our house was four houses down from the cutoff where I could ride the bus. So I was given my own house key. I didn't think I knew of any sevenyear-olds today that have their own house key. I would go to the neighbor's house in the morning when Mom left for work, and the neighbor lady would tell me when it was time to leave for school. At the end of the day, I walked home and let myself in. I spent about a half hour alone before my dad got home from work. By today's standards, you would probably judge my mother harshly. Today, it would probably border on child abuse or at least neglect. However, in 1962, people didn't look at it that way. I do not recall feeling neglected.

In the winter, my mom arranged for a taxicab to pick me up in the morning and take me to school. In the afternoon, the taxi would be waiting for me along with the buses to take me home. The seven-year-old me thought that was pretty cool. I have no idea what my classmates thought, but I'm sure they thought it very strange. Every Friday night, our routine was to do the weekly grocery shopping and stop by the cab company to pay for the following week's fares.

Every August, the factory where my dad worked shut down for two weeks. Mom would take vacation, and we would go to Florida to see my grandpa (my mom's dad). We drove because that's what families did for vacation. We always stopped two nights on the trip down and back. My grandpa lived in Orlando. I loved those trips. Mom would always arrange for us to take little side trips to take in various attractions. Our first night would be spent in either Gatlinburg or Chattanooga, Tennessee. There was always something fun to do there. The second night would be spent somewhere around the Georgia/Florida line, and we would arrive at Grandpa's house the third day. Mom took me to every attraction available between our house and Grandpa's house. I loved vacation!

One of the best parts happened toward the end of our trip. We would leave Grandpa's and head for Daytona Beach. We rented a larger room that had a kitchenette. Instead of eating out every night, Mom cooked our food. The water was where I wanted to be, either in the hotel pool or in the ocean. My mom would put her swimsuit on, but she wouldn't go in the water with me. I remember my dad rolling up his pants legs and wading into the ocean with me. After dark, he would put on his swim trunks and take me to the hotel pool after everyone else had gone to their rooms. He hated the way his legs looked and would never show them in public. But he would get in the pool after dark so I could swim.

When I was ten, I wanted to join Girl Scouts. However, none of the existing troops had room for me, or they met after school when I had no transportation to attend. My mom agreed to become a troop leader if my sister would help her. Our scout meetings were held in our basement on Saturday mornings. Carol would go to leader meetings while my mom was at work. Between the two of them, I was able to have a scouting memory.

By the time I was eleven, Mom decided that I could stay home by myself during summer break from school. Oh my gosh! The freedom I experienced was breathtaking. I could ride my bike anywhere I wanted. The neighborhood kids and I played from dawn until dark and sometimes after dark. You just can't play "ghost in the graveyard" during the day. I rode my bike to the library and borrowed books to pass the days. I even rode my bike to the public pool, which was about five miles away. I would let Mom know when I was going to the pool, and she would stop by on her way home from work to pick me. We would put my bike in the trunk, and I didn't have to pedal my bike home after swimming all day.

I remember Sunday summer afternoons when it would be so hot. Mom wouldn't feel like cooking, so we would have strawberries or peaches with shortcake for dinner. (I guess I should have realized why she only wanted to eat sugary food.)

My nieces were taking piano lessons, and I lamented that I would love to take piano lessons. What did Mom do? She bought a piano and signed me up for lessons. I never was very good at it, but it did lay the foundation for my taking up the clarinet in the school band. I must have driven her crazy with my playing because she signed me up for private clarinet lessons with the band director in the summer. She always made sure I had everything I needed to succeed. The only thing lacking really was help with my homework. Mother never helped with homework. I was to figure it out on my own. Looking back, I think it was probably because of her lack of confidence in her own education. She never graduated high school, only attending through the tenth grade.

By the time I was a teenager, I had joined the Rainbow Girls. If you aren't familiar with this organization, I certainly understand. It was a branch of the Masonic lodge for girls between the ages of thirteen and twenty. As I became more involved, Mom drove me all over the place to attend meetings and events. The happiest times of my youth were being part of the band, Rainbow Girls, and the church youth group. Although I wasn't allowed to do most of the things the other kids were doing, these three organizations provided an outlet for me from my home life.

Most of the time, it was just Mom and me. My dad had become an alcoholic by the time I was ten. He no longer bothered coming home after work, instead going straight to the bar. There were many days I never saw my dad. He was gone to work in the morning before I got up and didn't come home at night until after I was in bed. Regardless, my mom carried on as if nothing was wrong. She tried to make sure my life was as normal as possible.

I've mentioned already that my mom and I had some rough times during my growing up. Mother had a sharp tongue and never hesitated in using it. She said many hurtful things to me over the years. She was good at belittling me in front of others and trying to control my every move. However, I have to constantly return to some happy memories when the bad memories start clouding over. Mother could be generous when it suited her while in the next minute withholding love and acceptance. Living with Mother was a dichotomy that would follow me into adulthood. Caring for her through her dementia presented the same contradiction. One minute she could be sweet and personable and the next minute she would turn hateful and difficult. You are probably thinking I should have been used to it by then, but I think every child hopes there will come a day when you can be on an even footing with your parent. For me, we never really got to that point.

TWENTY-SIX

In 2003, my sister decided to come to Ohio for a visit. She and her husband planned to drive from Alaska to Ohio. Because they were both retired, they had all the time in the world to make the trip. Carol's thought was to come to Ohio, visit for a week, and then take Mom back to Alaska with her. On the trip back, they would stop in Colorado and Wyoming for short visits with her daughters, and so Mother could see her grandchildren and greatgrandchildren. Carol would have Mother for a week or so in Alaska and then fly her back to Ohio. She thought this would be a good way to give me a break from Mom and give Mom an opportunity to leave the confines of her apartment for a while. Carol was also hoping to visit an assisted living facility in her town to show Mom how nice it was. If Mom would see the place and Carol could convince her, we could move Mom to Alaska to live at the Manor. Carol could stop in to visit her but wouldn't have to do all the things I had been doing for Mom.

I was ecstatic. The thought of being free for a month (with the possibility for longer) was too much to believe, and, indeed, it was. The air escaped my balloon in one huge pop when Mom learned of the plans. At first, when Carol laid out the plan, Mom said she would think about it. That's when the trouble began. Whenever Mom thought about something too long, her mind would take control and contort her thoughts into darkness.

"Why is Carol coming to Ohio?"

"Like she told you, she's coming for a visit. She's hoping you will go back with her on the return trip so you can see the grandchildren and great-grandchildren."

"No, she has something else in mind. She'll get me up there and not let me come home."

"Mom, that is ridiculous. Of course, she will let you come home. She plans to fly you home when you are ready."

"I'm not falling for that. Once I get to Alaska, she won't let me come back."

"I don't know what I can say to you to make you believe otherwise. Don't you want to see Carol and Pete?

Wouldn't it be nice to get a break from me?"

"Why would I need a break from you?"

Unable to think of a comeback, I said, "Let's just wait until they get here, and you can discuss it with the two of them."

While Carol and Pete were in Ohio, they stayed with Pete's sister, who lived close to Mom. They visited with other family in the area and went to Mother's apartment almost daily. They got to experience the thrill of grocery shopping with Mother. They took her out for lunch. They even took her to Pete's sister's house for an afternoon. They tried everything to provide a change of scenery and routine for her. However, by the end of the week when they were ready to turn their vehicle west, Mom dug in her heels and refused to go with them. I often wonder what benefits we could all have enjoyed if she had only gone with them. Well, at least I got a little break for which I was thankful.

Breaks in the routine of caring for a dementia patient are always welcome. After my sister went back to Alaska, I still had my daughter and Uncle Ray. It was in the fall that year that Uncle Ray called me following one of Mother's routine doctor's appointment. The doctor wanted to discuss something with me, so I called the office. Dr. Birx told me that Mother's blood work indicated there might be a problem with her kidneys. He wanted to refer her to a nephrologist for some tests. I called Dr. Woods, the nephrologist, and scheduled a visit for Mother. I would have to take her to this doctor's visit. I needed more information. After an initial urinalysis, Dr. Woods told me Mother appeared to have some kidney failure. To get a better picture, he wanted to get a twenty-four-hour urine sample so he could measure output and look at some other factors. When he explained the procedure, I knew Mother was never going to be able to do this on her own. I was going to have to spend a full twenty-four hours with her in order to get this right.

I told my boss that I would be working remotely from Mom's house until we collected what we needed. I decided to begin the collection at 9:00 a.m. While Mother didn't enjoy peeing in a jug, she did not make a big fuss or give me any back talk. I was confused and thankful. When I arrived at Mom's the first day, I set up my computer on the kitchen table and logged into the office. After about ten minutes, I was so hot I was perspiring. I checked the thermostat to find the temperature in the apartment was 85 degrees. As any normal person would, I turned the thermostat down so the heat wouldn't kick on until the temperature reached at least 70 degrees. It was only October, not like the middle of winter. The sun was shining, which added more heat coming through the windows. I went back to my computer. Probably fifteen minutes later, I noticed Mother looking at the thermostat.

"Did you turn the thermostat down?"

"Yes. It's like an oven in here. Aren't you sweltering?"

"No. Just leave it alone. I like it warm. It will be cold in here in no time where you have it set."

"Okay. Could we maybe compromise? How about seventy-five instead of seventy? That will still be plenty warm."

"No. I like it at eighty-five. That's where I kept the heat when I was in Florida."

How well I remember, I thought to myself. She kept the air conditioner set at eighty-five as well. The air conditioner hardly ever kicked on, and when I visited, I would sit out in her breezeway in the swing trying to get some relief.

Well, if she wasn't going to compromise with the heat, I had a backup plan. I went into the bedroom, changed out of my blue jeans, and put on a pair of shorts with a T-shirt.

"Shorts! Don't you think it's a little cold to be wearing shorts?"

"Mother, it is so hot in here I can't even concentrate on my work. At least, this will help a little."

Throughout the day, I stepped outside for a few minutes to cool down. The temperature outside was in the sixties and felt so good.

Once we got past the temperature battle, the next battle became trying to get her to drink something, anything! She had coffee with her toast for breakfast, but I couldn't get her to drink any water. I tried filling a glass and sitting on the end table next to her chair. She took a couple of sips, but the amount in the glass had not diminished much by the evening. The jug we were supposed to be filling, about the size of a gallon milk jug, was not collecting much. By the following morning, we had probably only collected about a quart of liquid.

I got ready for work, said goodbye to Mom, and stopped by Dr. Woods's office to drop off the sample. The receptionist said they would call in a few days to schedule an appointment to go over the results. I had a sinking feeling those results would not be good. When I got the call and took Mother for the appointment, I was right. Dr. Woods said there was some kidney failure but that it would be quite some time before she needed dialysis. Her creatinine levels were higher than normal, and I explained to him how difficult it had been to get her to drink anything. He agreed that drinking water could help her tremendously but also acquiesced the point that she probably wouldn't change. We decided not to do anything at the present time and to continue monitoring her creatinine levels. Dr. Woods notified Dr. Birx, and we entered a holding pattern.

I tried to explain the situation to Mother, but her glassy-eyed look told me she wasn't comprehending the severity of the problem. She did agree to make an effort to drink more water. Every time I went to her house after that, I saw a glass sitting beside her chair. I checked it each time to see if it was a different glass. She could be just keeping it there to make me believe she was trying. There was no way to know.

TWENTY-SEVEN

Another year turned over on the calendar. By February, I was alarmed at the numbers and dates accumulating in my phone journal regarding Mother's medication. The pill caddy was empty, so she wasn't refilling that regularly. The number of pills in her bottles was not decreasing at a fast-enough rate. Without her blood pressure and cholesterol medications, she could have a heart attack. My worst fear was coming to her apartment and finding her on the floor. Attending to her once a week was not enough, but I didn't know how I could fit in other visits. In addition to a possible heart attack, I had to consider the possibility of falls. She hadn't exhibited a propensity for falls, but she wasn't getting any younger either.

I began searching online for help. Surely, there must be agencies that could help me take care of her. I figured the biggest problem would be money and the fact that she had none. I called some assisted living places, but the monthly rent was more than Mother received in four months. They did have a few rooms available for low-income residents, but there were long waiting lists and no guarantees when a room would become available. I felt like I was running out of time. Watching television one night, I saw an advertisement for a website, "help4seniors.org." Once again, God had provided.

From work the next day, I visited the website and found a phone number. The number turned out to be for the Council on Aging. They could certainly help me but would need to do an assessment of Mother to put a plan into place. They were also willing to make the appointment in the evening so I wouldn't have to take time off work. We scheduled the appointment. When I went to Mom's house, I explained to her what I was doing—that I was trying to get some help for her.

"I don't need any help," she quickly responded.

"Okay. You might not need help, but I do. How about that?"

"What do you need help with?"

"With you!" I tried not to scream.

"Why do you need help with me?"

"Mom, I can't be here all the time, and you need more assistance than I can provide. You aren't taking your medication. Your diet is atrocious. You could fall or become ill, and I wouldn't be here."

"I do, too, take my medication."

Without wanting to escalate this discussion further, I just carried on as if she hadn't said a word.

"A woman named Phyllis will be here tomorrow night at 6:00 p.m. I will get here as quickly as I can after work hopefully before she gets here."

Phyllis arrived at Mother's the next evening. I introduced myself and Mom. She sat down at Mom's kitchen table with her computer and began the interview. She knew Mother had dementia, but she continued to direct all the questions to her. Of course, Mom couldn't answer any of the questions correctly. I stepped in as delicately as possible to say those things weren't exactly true and to fill in with the correct answers. During the entire interview, Mom sat on the kitchen chair with one leg/foot folded up resting on the edge of the chair. Put her hair in a ponytail and a phone in her hand, she would have looked like a teenager with wrinkles. Phyllis looked at her in amazement. She couldn't believe Mother was able to sit like that. I agree that Mother was nimble. Her whole life, no one was ever able to guess her age correctly. However, appearing youthful belies the turmoil within, especially with her mind.

Phyllis concluded the interview, and I received the report a few days later. Phyllis's manager called to say that Mom did not qualify for a nursing home facility, but there were options available that could help her stay in her home a while longer. Are you kidding me? I thought to myself. I didn't want her staying in her home for a while longer. That was the whole point!

As I tried to focus on her words, she explained what they were going to do for Mom.

First on the list was applying for Medicaid. Once Medicaid was approved, and she had no doubt it would be; the agency would begin putting the rest of the plan into place. Once I had the letter of approval from Medicaid, I called the Council on Aging. By now, we were in summer. The first appointment would be someone coming to Mom's apartment to install an automated pill dispenser hooked up to her phone line. The dispenser would sound a bell when it was time for Mother to take her pills (talk about Pavlov's dog). If she didn't take her medication, she would get a call to ensure that she did. This sounded good to me. The person installing this would also be delivering a medical alert badge for Mom. If she fell or needed help at any time, all she had to do was press a button and paramedics would be dispatched to check on her. I wasn't sure she would wear it as a necklace, so I suggested a bracelet.

After everything was installed, I explained as clearly as possible to Mother what these things were for. She nodded her head appropriately, but I just wasn't sure she understood fully what she needed to do. I also explained to her that a person would be coming to her apartment every day with a meal. Another service provided by the agency was Meals on Wheels. They would have delivered three meals a day, but I wasn't sure she would even answer the door once a day. I told her she was going to have to answer the door for this person. I chose the dinner meal to be delivered three times a week. At least, one person would be seeing her now. I felt relieved for this extra contact.

Everything had been in place for a few days when I stopped by to attend to Mother's shopping and to see how she was doing with her new setup. Everything still seemed to be in place. She was still wearing the bracelet.

Praise God! I asked her if the Meals on Wheels people had delivered her dinner yet.

"Yes. A cute little girl has been stopping by with food."

"Oh, good," I replied. "What did you have for dinner?"

"I wasn't hungry, so I put it in the refrigerator."

Alarm bells went off in my head as I opened the refrigerator. I saw about four Styrofoam containers sitting on the top shelf. As I opened each container, I saw that none of the food had been eaten. "Mom, why haven't you eaten any of the food that's been delivered?"

"I did eat food."

"All of these containers have food in them. It looks like entire meals."

"No, it's not. I took out the fruit and cookies."

Sure enough, sitting in the center of the table were a banana, orange, and apple. I also saw empty packages of cookies and graham crackers.

"So you ate dessert but nothing else. Why? These meals look like food you would normally eat."

"Well, that just wasn't what I wanted to eat at the time."

"Mom, this is a giant waste of food if you aren't going to eat what they provide."

"I didn't ask for it."

"I know you didn't ask for it, but I'm trying to help you here."

Changing the subject abruptly, she declared, "Let's go to the store. I want to see what kind of flowers are on sale this week."

I swear she had the attention span of a gnat and the mind of a four-year-old. Off to the store we went. The heck with food, we needed to see what flowers were on sale!

We progressed on with the Meals on Wheels. Over time, she did eat some of the food delivered. The biggest benefits, in my opinion, were the visits from another person.

TWENTY-EIGHT

Over the months, things deteriorated again. One visit, she wasn't wearing her bracelet.

"What happened to your alert bracelet?"

"My what?"

"The bracelet you were wearing."

"Oh. I got tired of it and took it off."

"What did you do with it?"

"I don't know. It's around here somewhere."

Keeping calm, I quietly reminded her of the purpose of the bracelet. The alert would let me know if something happened to her.

"Nothing has happened to me yet, has it?"

"No. We've been very blessed. But that doesn't mean nothing will ever happen to you."

"I suppose."

"So would you please put it back on?"

"If I find it."

On another visit, I checked her pill dispenser to fill it. The dial didn't turn, and I was trying to figure out what happened. I traced the power cord to the wall only to find it had been unplugged.

"Mom, why is your pill dispenser unplugged?"

"It kept beeping and was annoying."

"When it beeps, you are supposed to take your medication. Does anyone call you about your pills?"

"Some woman calls me about every day. I finally stopped answering the phone."

I checked the answering machine. Sure enough, it contained multiple messages regarding taking her pills.

"Okay. Let's try this again. I am going to refill your pill dispenser and plug it back into the wall. When you hear the beep, please take your pills. You have to take your medication every day. Do you understand?"

"Yes."

But she didn't. I don't know whether it was an understanding problem or a stubbornness problem. I kept at it, trying to use these tools to care for her. I don't know if she wasn't capable of complying or if it was because I was the one trying to get her to comply. If Mother didn't want to do something, she wasn't going to do it. Period. The struggle continued for months. Upon visiting one evening, I went to refill her pills, and the dispenser was gone.

"Mom! Where is the pill dispenser?"

"The what?" She was busy watching television.

"The big round disk that was sitting here?"

"Oh, that thing. I just got tired of the beeping and unplugged it."

"But where is it?"

"I put it in the bedroom closet."

I went to her closet and couldn't find it. I then went to the spare room, found it sitting there on top of some boxes, and brought it back out to the dining area. I didn't even bother trying to plug it back in. Instead, I just started crying.

With tears streaming down my cheeks, I sat down on the couch across from her.

"Why are you crying?"

Almost whispering, I said, "I can't do this anymore. You fight everything I'm trying to do to help you."

"What?"

Strength returning to my voice, I dried the tears and said, "Mom, the time has come for you to move to a nursing home. This living on your own is not working, and it is dangerous for you. I have to make sure you are safe, and the only way for me to do that is by moving you to a safer location."

She just looked at me. There was no hostility, no comprehension, no awareness.

"Just do whatever you need to do."

"I am. You need twenty-four-hour care, and I cannot provide that. I will call around and see what I can find out, what the next steps are, and how we can move forward. I want you to be safe. I love you, and I need to know that you are all right."

The next day, I began looking into nursing homes.

TWENTY-NINE

You might be tempted to think that admitting someone to a nursing home is a relatively easy thing to do. Well, you would be wrong. Just because I knew Mom needed to be moved didn't make it so. The first thing I learned is that Mom had to be referred for nursing care, either by her doctor or social agency. I thought I would start with her doctor. He had been attending her for over six years. Surely, he would give me the referral I needed. I scheduled an appointment for Mom and went with her this time. Dr. Birx said he didn't feel comfortable making that referral. To him, Mom seemed perfectly fine. I had to question Dr. Birx's mental capability at this point. Had he not been paying attention over the past six years? What? Did Mom just show up and he just renewed her prescriptions without even noticing her decline? So I asked him.

"Do you agree that she has dementia?"

"Yes, she definitely has dementia, but in my opinion, she doesn't require a nursing home."

"Dr. Birx, I have met with the Council on Aging. She has been evaluated." I further explained everything I had been doing to try to help her over the past year.

"Well, then, you should keep doing what you're doing."

"But she doesn't cooperate!"

"Sounds like she's a little stubborn." He chuckled.

My face felt afire. I thanked Dr. Birx for his time and hurriedly left his office with Mother in tow. I dropped Mom at home and immediately called the Council on Aging again. I explained where we were with the "trying to keep Mom in her home" idea. I explained my devastating appointment with Dr. Birx. I was on the verge of tears again when the woman said we should set up another assessment for Mom. The council was able to refer people to nursing homes, and they would be more than willing to do that for me depending on Mom's new assessment. I expressed my concern given the results of the last assessment. The woman assured me a different social worker would be assessing Mom this time. Interesting, I thought. We scheduled a new day and time for a new assessment.

Vicky was our new social worker. On the day of the appointment, I happened to pull into Mother's parking lot at the same time as she was parking her car. I introduced myself and explained my reluctance over this assessment. Vicky let slip that Phyllis had been "let go" from the agency based on a number of assessments. Hope began to sprout in my chest. Could it be that Phyllis didn't know how to do her job and that Vicky had been sent here by God to get it right this time?

Vicky and I entered Mom's apartment, and I introduced her to Mother. We sat at the same kitchen table, with Vicky at her computer, and answered the same questions we had answered before. I showed Vicky the equipment I had tried and explained how Mother was unable to use the equipment. I showed her the Meals on Wheels food sitting in Mother's refrigerator. After she had gathered all her information, Vicky said goodbye to Mom and started for the door. Her eyes told me she wanted me to follow, so I explained to Mom I would walk Vicky to her car and be back in a minute.

As we walked, Vicky apologized for the poor result we had gotten the year before when contacting the agency.

"Clearly, your mother needs to be moved to a nursing home. I can't believe you've been struggling like this for a year."

"I felt like I needed to give it some time."

"Honey, you gave it more time than it deserved. You should have called us earlier. We would have sent someone out immediately to do a reassessment."

"I had no idea. I didn't want to get Phyllis in trouble, but I just felt like her assessment was wrong."

"You needn't have worried about Phyllis. Next time, go with what your gut is telling you." She smiled. "Don't let anyone say you haven't done everything humanly possible for your mother. Now, it's time to let someone else take on that responsibility. I will turn in my report in the morning, and you will be getting a call about the next steps. In the meantime, you should start looking at nursing homes."

I could have skipped all the way back to Mom's apartment if I thought that was possible. How long had it been since I'd skipped? As usual, I called my sister on my way home to give her the good news. I disagree with Janis Joplin. "Freedom [isn't] just another word for nothin' left to lose." Freedom is having a huge burden lifted from you, hauled away, and replaced with joy. Hopelessness replaced with happiness. I had new purpose, a new goal.

Within a few days, I had the paperwork I needed from the Council on Aging. I had narrowed the nursing home list down to two. I wanted to give Mother a choice, but I didn't want to overwhelm her with too many choices. I took a vacation day in order to visit the two nursing homes with Mom. I wasn't too surprised when she didn't fight me on this because I knew without a doubt that God was in control.

The first nursing home was a fairly new facility about halfway between my office and my home. One of the employees gave a tour of the facility, showing us one of the residents' rooms, the dining room, recreation facility, etc. Mom nodded along and smiled, but there was no real spark that told me this is where she wanted to be.

The second nursing home was in Cincinnati. It would mean a further drive for me but certainly manageable. The benefit was that my daughter worked at this nursing home. In my heart, this is really where I wanted Mom to be. Lynn would be able to visit with her occasionally. We met with the administrator, Debbie, who gave us the tour. The nursing home was run by Carmelite nuns. In addition, some retired nuns lived on the first floor. The building had three floors, with the top floor designated for Alzheimer's disease and dementia patients. At St. Margaret Hall (SMH), Mom could have a private room. She would have had to share a room with another woman at the other facility. On one floor, there was an aviary with multiple birds in residence. Another floor housed a giant aquarium with beautifully diverse fish. We went outdoors to find a courtyard nestled in between the wings of the building, with patio tables and chairs. I loved it and felt it would be perfect for Mother. However, I tried to quell my excitement. She needed to decide which facility suited her best.

After the tours, while driving home, I asked Mom, "So what did you think? Did either of the places look good to you?"

"Well, they were both nice, but I think I like the last one best. I liked the birds."

Again, trying not to appear too excited (if she thought it was my idea, she might not go with it), I calmly stated, "That was my favorite too." I then began pointing out all the advantages of having her own room, the wonderful courtyard, the chapel, everything.

"I think I will like it there."

"I think you will too."

"When am I moving?"

"Well, it's going to take me a little bit of time to put all of the pieces into place, but I will get started on it right away."

"Okay. Can we go to the store now?"

PART IV

THIRTY

Now that we had decided upon the place for Mother to live, I had even more work ahead of me. Once you decide on a facility, you can't just pack the truck and move in. My daughter introduced me to the nursing home director, Debbie, and we scheduled a time to get started on the next steps. Because I originally applied for Medicaid for Mother in Montgomery County and the nursing home was in Hamilton County, the first thing would be to apply for Medicaid in Hamilton County. I never realized that each county had their own Medicaid programs. I thought it was by state. Still learning something new every day. When I met with Debbie, I brought my "mother" file with me. From the fiasco in Florida, I had begun keeping everything relating to Mother in its own "expandable" file, and it seemed the file was expanding every day! Debbie was a little impressed I was so organized. What can I say? Over thirty years as a legal secretary, organization is how you survive.

Debbie took the Medicaid information I had and filled out the new application for Hamilton County. What a relief not to have to do that again! During the course of our conversation, Debbie gave me a to-do list—tasks I would have to complete before Mother could move. Likewise, she had her own to-do list based on the information I had given her regarding Mom. The meeting was so very productive, and, for once, I felt like the "establishment" was helping rather than hindering.

The first item on my list was to make Mother's funeral arrangements. While I did not consider Mother having much money, she could only have $1,500 in her name when she entered the nursing home under Medicaid.

As I recall, she probably had about $5,000 in assets. She also had a whole-life insurance policy that I would have to cash out. The face amount of the policy was $3,000, but she had not kept up with the monthly payments, so the cashout value would only be about $1,500. With an idea of how much money I needed to dump, I began looking for funeral homes. Mom had indicated during the more lucid time of her life that she wanted to be cremated. This would certainly be less expensive than a full-blown funeral with casket, viewing, and service. She did not have the money for any of that. After weighing my options with cremation, I contacted the funeral home in the city where I grew up. If we had the money and decided on a viewing year down the road, this would be convenient for those in Ohio who knew Mom. I met with the funeral director, made all the arrangements, and paid for all of it on the spot. The money would be invested into an annuity by the funeral home and would probably grow a little interest depending on when Mom died. If Mom survived for a while and the annuity grew interest, I would have more funds available at the time of her death to make some upgrades. After the funeral was taken care of, I called Debbie to let her know of my progress. I faxed the paperwork to her for Mom's file.

Next on my list was to take Mom shopping. Emily, from the finance office at SMH, provided me with suggestions for spending Mom's money down. I could gift it to her grandchildren. I could buy clothing and/or other accessories for Mom. (I apologize to the grandchildren here.) I just thought I should spend the money on Mom. She didn't have a whole lot of money to spend, but she probably didn't have long on this earth either. I thought I needed to do as much as I could for her. She was giving up all freedom by moving to the nursing home, and I knew that was not going to be easy for any of us.

I decided on a diversion tactic for the shopping trip. I had arranged with Mom to be at her house on Saturday morning but didn't tell her we were going shopping. When I arrived, we had a cup of coffee together, and I explained that we needed to evaluate what items of furniture she would like to take with her to the nursing home. Because she had a private room, we would have more space to accommodate a few of her favorite things to make it feel more like home. That was my thought anyway.

Surprisingly, she did not "cop an attitude" or give me any problems with this procedure. (In case you still aren't convinced, prayer works!) The first item she wanted, of course, was her recliner. She asked about her African violets, but, unfortunately, the nursing home did not allow residents to have plants. I told her I would find them a good home. I was shocked when she said she would ask her neighbor if she'd like to have them. First, she was willing to give something to another human being. Second, she had actually developed some sort of relationship with her next-door neighbor. I was truly amazed. What else did she do that I didn't know about?

We would obviously take her television and television stand. She asked if she could take her rocking chair, which I agreed would be an extra seat for visitors. She looked at me skeptically about that one. I could read her mind, "What visitors?" We then progressed to the bedroom. She asked if she could take her bed, but I had to tell her no. The nursing home wanted her to use their bed (a hospital bed) to make it easier for them to care for her. I suggested she take her dresser and chest of drawers. She said the dresser would be enough. She didn't think she needed the chest of drawers. God had clearly made the path straight here. There was no other explanation for her cooperation. I asked her to please go through her closet and drawers over the course of the next week to pick out the items of clothing and other personal items she wanted to take with her. With God in charge here, I thought it might be possible. It wasn't. More on that later. I then asked her if she'd like to do a little shopping.

"I thought maybe we could get you a few items of new clothing to take with you."

Her eyes lit up as she exclaimed, "Yes. That would be nice."

I took her to her favorite store, JCPenney. I thought we could spend a couple of hours there easily without having to shop the entire mall. We walked the entire women's department, looking at everything, but she wasn't picking anything out.

"Do you see anything you like?"

"Oh, I see lots of things I like."

"Well, you need to let me know. I haven't passed my 'mind reading' class yet." (She didn't get the joke.) So we started through the women's department again. When I saw things that caught my eye, I would ask her about it. Then we started making some progress. We managed to pick out a few pairs of new slacks and tops.

"I could use some new underwear."

"That's perfect! Let's head over to lingerie."

"Maybe some new pajamas too."

"We can do that too."

Once I got the ball rolling for her, she finally was able to pick out things on her own. In my mind, we were finished.

"What's upstairs?"

"It's just housewares and stuff."

"Can we go look?"

Visions of grocery shopping flashed across my mind, and I was afraid I was going to be at the mall all day. However, I decided to let her browse. She had so little in life. If a trip to JCPenney to browse brightened her day, then that's what we would do. We walked through every inch of the second floor, and then she was actually ready to go. I dropped her off at home with her new purchases and reminded her about going through her closet and drawers. She said she would.

THIRTY-ONE

Once all the tasks were checked off the list, it was time to move Mom at last. Her move-in was scheduled for March 20, 2008, the first day of spring. Ohio springs can be rather volatile, but Mother Nature cooperated and gave us a gorgeous rain-free day in which to move. Ben and I took the day off work, and Michael was on spring break from college, so he came to help too. I drove my car, and Ben followed in his truck. On arriving at Mom's apartment, she wasn't ready (of course). She hadn't packed anything that I'd asked her to take care of. Ben and Michael began loading her furniture on the truck while I packed her personal belongings. Thankfully, she wasn't able to move the entire apartment, and the things we were taking could be moved in one trip. This was especially good news as we had to travel around 50 miles from her apartment to the nursing home. Mother rode with me, and I tried to keep talking to keep her mind off things. She was very quiet, so it was a gargantuan task for me to talk to her for an hour.

A very nice man met us at the loading door and supplied us with a couple of carts on which we could transport Mother's things from the basement to the third floor. Thank you, Otis, for inventing elevators! Debbie met us on the third floor and introduced us to the nurses on the day shift. They were all so nice and warmly welcomed Mom. I just wish she had been a little nicer to them. I apologized as I was leaving and was told not to worry in the least. Apparently, they were used to that kind of behavior. I still felt sad that they had to endure that every day.

In no time at all, we had Mom set up in her new place. She had a nice big window that overlooked a city park with plenty of blooming trees and flowers. There was also a plethora of squirrels to keep her entertained. I unpacked Mother's clothes, filling her drawers and the closet. Somehow, we had managed to bring just enough, and I didn't need to take anything back with me. Michael set up Mom's television and cable. He excelled at that sort of thing. I thought her room looked cozy and inviting by the time we left.

A couple of days later, I went to see Mom. I didn't want to wait too long before stopping in so she wouldn't feel like she was just dumped there and forgotten. It was a beautiful Sunday afternoon, and I thought maybe I'd take her down to the courtyard and we could sit outside for a little while. When I got to her room, she wasn't there. I didn't think it was mealtime, so I inquired at the nurses' station. The nurses didn't know where she was either but told me she liked to visit the aviary in the basement. Off to the basement I went. I found the aviary, but Mother was nowhere in sight. Beginning to feel a little panicky, I walked the entire basement floor and then headed back up the elevator. Maybe we just passed each other in the air.

This time, when I got to her room, I found her sitting in her recliner in front of the television.

"Well, it's about time!" she said to me.

"What? What do you mean it's about time?"

"I've been waiting for you for days."

"I never gave you a specific day when I was coming to visit."

"Not to visit! I was waiting for you to come and take me home."

"Mom, this is your home. We moved you from the apartment into here because you needed help taking care of yourself."

"I don't need anyone to take care of me. I manage just fine on my own. Have all my life."

Obviously, this wasn't going well, and I needed to figure out quickly how to turn the conversation around.

Instead of arguing with her about the need for help, I walked over to the window.

"Oh, look, a couple of squirrels are playing in the tree. Have you watched them much?"

She walked over to stand next to me. "Yeah, they have a ball jumping from tree to tree. I think one of them is building a nest in that tree. Do you see it?"

I looked closely and couldn't see any nest, but I agreed anyway. "Oh, I see it. They will probably be having babies soon then, and you will have even more entertainment. I was thinking maybe we could go downstairs and sit in the courtyard for a little while, get some fresh air."

"You and your fresh air. You'd think you were raised in a barn or something as much time as you spend outdoors."

"So would you like to try it?"

"No. It's too chilly."

"That's too bad. It's a beautiful day, about 75 degrees and sunny. There wouldn't be any wind in the courtyard because the building surrounds it."

"Maybe some other time."

"Okay. Maybe next week."

I tried to keep up a conversation, but it's really difficult when the person on the other end won't help keep it going. After an hour, I was ready for a straitjacket. I stood to leave.

"Well, I think I'm going to take off. I have some yard work to do, and I have to get ready for work tomorrow."

"Okay. I'll walk you out."

"You really don't need to do that."

"I don't mind. It will be dinner time soon anyway."

I looked at the clock. It was 2:00 p.m. However, I didn't fight it. We rode the elevator to the basement again and walked the hallway to the back door of the facility. There was a nice parking lot for family and employees. I hugged Mom and told her I'd be back soon then quickly left so she didn't have time to think about that comment. I didn't look back, just went straight to my car. I pretended to adjust my rearview mirror and saw that she was still standing there. I drove off without waving or acknowledging that she was still there. I didn't want to do anything that would encourage her to open that door and walk out.

In the past seven years I'd been caring for her, Mother had not wandered away. I did not think she was a flight risk and had said as much to the staff when I signed her up to live there. I was assured they would keep an eye on her, and if it appeared she was going to be a problem, they would put a monitor on her. I very much hoped it wouldn't come to that. I wanted her life to remain as normal as she thought it was. Tears came as I drove home. I knew it was unrealistic, but I still felt guilty for moving her there. The accumulation of all the reasons I moved her there didn't matter. I argued with myself and talked to God all the way home. By the time I turned on the driveway, I felt peaceful. Regardless, I just knew I wasn't past the guilt feelings just yet. They would come back at some point.

THIRTY-TWO

My sister and brother-in-law arrived in Ohio the first weekend of April. They had had so much fun with me moving Mother from Florida to Ohio that they came to help me empty her apartment. (If that didn't sound sarcastic, it was meant to be.) As usual, they stayed with Pete's sister a couple of miles from Mom's apartment. I had paid the rent through the end of April, but I didn't want to put it off until the end of the month. It didn't matter to me if the apartment sat empty for a few weeks on my dime.

The great thing about them staying with Pete's sister was that her husband always lent them his truck while they visited. His truck together with Ben's truck gave us double the capacity for hauling things away. We decided to give ourselves the weekend to relax and visit family and start the cleanup on Monday. Late on Sunday afternoon, I took Carol and Pete to the nursing home to visit Mother. I tried to time the visit so we would have about forty-five minutes with her before it was mealtime. Mother never missed mealtime even if she didn't eat very much. I reasoned this would make it easier for us to leave.

The three of us walked into her room and greeted her. She looked from me to Pete to Carol. Instead of a return greeting, we received a scowl instead. Carol didn't miss a beat. She walked over to Mom and tried to hug her. I say "tried" because Mother just stood there stiff as a board and did not hug her back. Carol was still not deterred.

"You have a really nice room here, Mother." No response.

"I love this big window," she said, crossing the room. "That's a nice park next door. Nice pathways to walk on. It even has picnic tables. Maybe we can bring a picnic one day while we are here and take you over there." No response.

Carol then went over and sat on Mom's bed. I let Pete have the rocking chair, and I sat on Mom's footstool. Carol chattered on about all kinds of things. I still don't know how she did it. She always was good at conversation even with total strangers. She's the extrovert and I'm the introvert. It's not as easy for me. After about thirty minutes of this, I chimed in and suggested we give Carol and Pete a tour of the facility.

We went to the second floor and found the aquarium with all the brightly colored fish. The room had huge windows that residents could look out and watch the birds in the trees. Then we went to the first floor and I showed them the chapel. The sun was streaming through the stained-glass windows engulfing the space with warm, muted light. I also showed them the office space where my daughter worked. It being Sunday, no one was in the office, but we could look in through the door.

From there, we went to the basement, and Mother went directly to the aviary. This had become her favorite place to visit. She finally thawed out and excitedly showed us all the birds. She talked about the birds in the little birdhouses and the nests they had made. She had been watching for babies but hadn't seen any yet. We walked down the hall and out into the courtyard where tulips were blooming. We walked along the pond, but they didn't have the fountain going yet, probably waiting to make sure it didn't freeze again. After all this, I remarked that we had better get Mother to the dining room as dinner would be starting soon. We had to walk past the dining room to get to the back door to the parking lot.

"I'll walk you to the door."

"It's okay. I don't want you to be late for dinner."

"I won't be late. They haven't even started setting out the food yet."

"Okay."

We all said our goodbyes and "I love yous." I mentioned to them as we walked across the parking lot about not turning back toward the door, to just keep walking. It did seem to make the leaving easier for her if I did this each time. As we were pulling out of the lot, I noticed she was not standing at the door but was walking toward the dining room. I said a silent thank you to God.

Monday morning, we had agreed to meet at Mother's at 9:00 a.m. Ben and I arrived about eight thirty, and Carol and Pete were already there. I guess I didn't have to worry about them sleeping in. They had been able to catch up on their rest over the weekend. The flight from Alaska to Ohio is grueling, and it really does take you about a day to get your bearings.

As I had the key, they couldn't get in until I got there. We agreed to remedy that immediately. I gave them Mom's key so we would both have one. That way if they wanted to get started before we arrived, they would be able to get in. I started a pot of coffee while we discussed where to begin. My sister and I agreed that we were going to go through all of Mother's belongings. There was no sense throwing the baby out with the bath water. We wanted to treat her things with respect. After all, not everything was junk, and we believed we would find some things that we would want to keep and things our children and grandchildren might like to have.

With our cups of coffee, we decided to start in the spare bedroom. The closet was packed full with all the stuff we moved from Florida. Carol and I started on the closet while Ben and Pete took the spare bed apart and put it in one of the pickup trucks. Goodwill wouldn't take beds or furniture, but the Salvation Army would. Once we had both trucks loaded, I would show them how to get to the store. We created three piles—one for the Salvation Army, one for things we wanted to keep, and one for the dumpster. As we added items to the Army and dumpster piles, Ben and Pete would start carrying them out.

By lunchtime, we had cleaned out the entire spare room, and the trucks were full enough to go to the Army.

"You, guys, follow us. After we off-load everything, we can pick up some fast-food for lunch. How does Wendy's sound?"

"We like Wendy's," my sister replied. "I'd like to get a Frosty!"

"Me too!"

Back at the apartment, we ate our lunch and decided we would spend the afternoon cleaning out Mother's bedroom. Carol started on the cedar chest, and I began in the closet. In case I didn't mention this at the beginning of the story, our Mother was a hoarder. I think I counted thirty shoeboxes. Now, I understand some people use shoeboxes to store other things in, but when it came to our mom, every box contained a pair of shoes. She had a thing for shoes and dishes. I inherited the dish thing as I love dishes. My daughter inherited the shoe thing as she has about the same number of pairs as her grandmother.

We quickly discovered this room was going to take us much longer than the spare room. The cedar chest was full to the brim with memorabilia. Carol would find a treasure, and I would have to stop and take a look. We found things from my childhood that Mother had saved. We also found many items from the 1940s. Mom worked the assembly line at a plant called Brown & Brockmeyer during the war. It was noisy, monotonous work, but she made good money. We found some of her pay stubs. We also found ration books, one of which was still intact and never been used. The chest contained scrapbooks from that time and what seemed like millions of pictures. Instead of taking the time to look at every picture, we decided to put them all in boxes and take them to my house. I could then go through them at a later time and decide if there was anything worth keeping.

By five, we were all tired and ready for dinner. We decided to meet at 8:00 a.m. the next day and get an earlier start. The empty cedar chest (we had packed the contents into boxes) and Mom's couch went onto Ben's truck to take to our house. Carol had found a prayer book that belonged to our grandmother, Mom's mother, and she took that with her to look through that evening. It probably wasn't going to be feasible for Carol to take much of anything home with her as she was flying although she found a few small things that she wanted to have that would fit in her suitcase.

The next day, we finished up in Mom's bedroom. We called around to see if any other family members might be interested in her bed and chest of drawers. Finding no takers, we loaded them on the truck to give to the Salvation Army. We now had two rooms empty and moved on to the kitchen. While Carol and I worked there, Pete unloaded the hall linen closet, and Ben worked on the medicine cabinet in the bathroom. The first thing we did was pull all the dishes out of the cabinets and stacked everything on the living room floor. Carol thought we should call Uncle Ray and Aunt Charlotte to see if they were interested in having anything. Aunt Charlotte found a couple of glass pieces she wanted. One less trip to the Salvation Army!

From the cabinets, we opened the pantry. We found canned goods we had moved from Florida seven years earlier. All that went into the garbage bags for the dumpster. One shelf contained plastic containers from the salad bar and deli at the grocery store. Consider I took her to the grocery once a week for seven years, that's how many plastic containers were stored in the pantry. We found bottles of liquor that we moved from Florida still gathering dust. She had never had one drink from them. We still don't know why she kept them. Fond memories, maybe?

Who knows? However, they all went down the drain. Ben said none of it would be any good after sitting for so long. We couldn't even tempt him with the whiskey we found.

By the end of the second day, we felt like we were closing in on the end. On Wednesday, we finished the last little bits and cleaned the place. With one final look, we locked the door and said goodbye to Mother's apartment. Her life was becoming smaller and smaller. A great deal of items made their way to my house to be stored in our barn until I could go through it all. She had decades' worth of receipts, tax returns, pay stubs, and other paper. I kept some of her clothing, especially her winter clothes, in case she wanted/needed it come the fall. I didn't know why, but I held onto sheets and blankets. I kept way more than was necessary. I just didn't know and felt rather overwhelmed. I decided to give myself some time and space to sort through it all. As we pulled out of the parking lot for the last time, I stopped at the office and handed in Mother's keys. This chapter was finished.

THIRTY-THREE

The weekend came, and I invited Carol and Pete, along with Pete's sister and husband, to my house for dinner on Saturday. I decided to turn it into a festive occasion to celebrate all the hard work we'd done during the week. One of the things I kept of Mom's was her china. In the seventies, Mom was involved in Eastern Star (a branch of the Masonic lodge). She rose to the position of worthy matron in 1974. During this time, people were always buying her gifts for one reason or another, so she decided to start the china collection. She had always wanted a set of china but never had the money for it. She started a gift registry, and people could purchase pieces for her set, much like a bridal registry. To my knowledge, Mother never used the china. She had eight place settings and several serving pieces, but they sat in boxes. I still didn't understand the desire for the china if she did not intend to ever use it. It wasn't even displayed in a hutch or anything so she could at least admire it. She moved the boxes from Ohio to Florida and back again.

I took the boxes home and washed all the pieces and made room for them in my china hutch. On this celebratory occasion, I decided we would use Mother's china for our dinner. I also saved some of her prettier glassware and included that in the place settings. Years before, Mom had given me her silver. I used it all the time for special occasions, and we used that for our dinner too. Carol and I joked about how horrified Mother would be if she knew we were using her finest things for our dinner. I think we felt like a couple of naughty children getting away with something behind Mother's back. A piece of me felt guilty. Mom was sitting in a nursing home, and we were enjoying our freedom and her things—a dichotomy that lived with me often.

Dinner was wonderful as we talked and laughed. We all felt as if a burden had been lifted. I no longer had to worry about Mom. I knew she was in very capable hands. I knew she would get healthy food (if she would eat it). She would get her medications every day. People were looking after her on an hourly basis to make sure she was safe. The burden of her well-being was no longer mine.

Carol and Pete still had a week before their return flight to Alaska. I had to return to work as I had only taken a week's "vacation" time. They were able to visit with Aunt Charlotte and Uncle Ray. Even our cousins found time to visit with them. Carol wanted to spend as much time as she could with Mom before she left since she didn't know when they would make it back to Ohio again. However, Carol didn't want to go see Mom every day. This would have been a little more than anyone could handle. Instead, they made the trips a couple of days and used my tactic of visiting near mealtime.

One sunny day, Carol decided to bring a picnic and take Mom to the park as she had promised the week before. She called Mom before making the trip to Cincinnati to see what she might like for lunch. Mom wanted Wendy's. What can I say? All of us are suckers for a Frosty! Carol and Pete went through a drive-through on the way. Arriving at the nursing home, Mother was surprised to see them.

Not missing a beat, Carol said, "We thought you might like to visit the park next door. We brought Wendy's for lunch."

"Did you get me a Frosty?"

"Of course! We also brought you a bacon cheeseburger."

"I like those. Any fries?"

"Yep."

"Okay."

By the conversation, you would think they hadn't talked in weeks instead of an hour or so prior. Carol and I learned over the years not to ask her constantly if she remembered conversations or events. She didn't and constantly asking her caused her frustration. She had no idea she wasn't remembering everything that happened in a day. In her mind, life was normal, and she had no memory issues.

Off to the park they went.

"They even have picnic tables!" Mother exclaimed.

"I know. Look, they even have grills if people would like to grill their food here. You didn't see this from your room window?"

"No. I just watch the squirrels." (Mom was so observant.)

"Here's a nice table in the shade. It's getting a little warm." (My sister can't handle any temperature above 60 degrees, and God help us if there is humidity.)

"If we sit in the shade, I'm going to need a sweater."

"Mother, it's 75 degrees out here."

"But it's not seventy-five in the shade."

"Okay. We will sit in the sun for a little bit," Carol said begrudgingly.

In the meantime, Pete had found a table that met both requirements. Part of the table was in the sun and the rest of it was shaded. Perfect! Until it wasn't.

After eating, the three of them strolled around the park for a little while.

"I guess we'd better get you back to your room. Pete and I need to head back before the traffic gets bad on the Interstate."

"So when are you taking me back home?"

"Mom, this is your home. Where would you go 'back' to?"

"This isn't my home. I want to go back to Florida. Diane brought me up. Now, I want to go back."

"First of all, Diane didn't bring you up here against your will. It was a decision made by all of us. You told Diane you wanted to come back to Ohio, so we all moved you to Ohio. Second of all, there is nothing to go back to. Your place in Florida doesn't exist anymore. This is where you live now."

They walked back to Mom's room in angry silence. Carol tried to hug Mom and told her she loved her.

Nothing from Mom.

"We will be back in a few days for another visit before we head back to Alaska."

"Don't bother." Mom pouted.

"Well, maybe you'll change your mind. We'll see you soon."

On the weekend, I decided to go with Carol to see Mom. We decided on lunch. By now, you may think the only thing our family does is eat. Not really, but we found over the years it was easier to get through a visit with Mother if we had something else to do besides just trying to talk to her. If we centered our visits around a meal, the silences weren't as awkward. We picked Mom up in her room and told her we were going to walk down the street to a pub on the corner for lunch.

"You might want to put some walking shoes on," I noted.

"These are fine. I'm walking in them now, aren't I?"

"Yes, but it's a little further to the corner than just walking around here." She pulled a different pair of loafers from her closet.

"You don't have anything like gym shoes?"

"No."

"Do we need to buy you a pair?"

"What for? I don't go anywhere. I'm stuck in this hellhole you put me in. I don't need any gym shoes." So this is how lunch was going to go.

"I want to go see the birds."

"Aren't you getting hungry?"

"Not really. I want to see if any of the babies are in the nests. We can stop on the second floor, and I can show you the fish."

"Mom, we've all see the fish a couple of times now. How about if we just go check on the baby birds?"

Off to the basement we traipsed. We must have looked like the pied piper and his followers. Unfortunately, none of the nests in the aviary produced any baby birds. None of the birds seemed to be too active, which disappointed Mom.

"Oh, well. I guess they are all sleeping. We might as well go wait for the dining room to open."

"Mom, we aren't going to the dining room. We thought we would take you out for lunch. There is a cute little pub down on the corner we thought we could try." Haven't we just been talking about this? Sometimes,

I wondered at how my head did not spin off my shoulders when trying to converse with her.

"Okay. I guess that would be okay."

Carol and I just looked at each other in desperation.

At the pub, we found a table by the front window where we could people-watch and enjoy the sunshine. Mom didn't know what she wanted for lunch. Carol practically read the entire menu to her, and she still couldn't make up her mind. Finally, she decided the egg salad sandwich might be good. We placed our order and tried to converse with Mom while we waited for our food. Carol chatted about all her children and grandchildren, which passed the time until our food arrived. We really thought Mom would have been more interested. These were her grandchildren and great-grandchildren after all. I was interested.

After nibbling at her food, Mom was more interested in the dessert menu. The pub had homemade pies, and she was very interested in having a piece of cherry pie. Although she couldn't eat all her sandwich, she had no problem licking the pie plate clean. We paid the bill and exited the dark pub into the bright sunlight.

"Where did you park the car?" Mom asked.

"We didn't drive, Mom. We walked."

"How far is it?"

"It's just at the top of this little hill. See?"

"I can't walk up that hill."

"Mom, it's not that far, and the hill is just a gradual incline."

"I'm too tired. I can't walk all that way."

While this conversation was happening, we were walking toward the nursing home. "Look! We're halfway there already. I think you can make it the rest of the way." Grumpily, she kept moving, and we were back in no time.

"See? That wasn't so bad. You made it all the way!"

She just glared at me as we entered in the nursing home. Safely ensconced in her room, we said our goodbyes and suggested she might like to take a nap after all that exercise. We were joking, but I'm sure she was asleep in her chair before we even made it to the parking lot.

THIRTY-FOUR

In May, the law firm I worked for merged with a mega law firm. The mega firm was based in Cincinnati with offices across Ohio, Kentucky, West Virginia, and Pennsylvania. I learned that if I wanted to remain employed with the newly merged firm, I would have to work out of the Cincinnati office. Everyone else from my prior firm remained in Dayton. The commute was not the issue as I actually lived in between the two cities. The drive time was very similar. The problem was I had to leave all my friends and coworkers. I had worked in Dayton for over twenty years. Now, I was going to have to start all over in a new-to-me city, making new friends and trying to fit into an IT department that didn't seem to be too happy with my arrival. The shining star in all this was the close proximity to St. Margaret Hall. I could make it to see Mom on my lunch hours, which meant I didn't have to stay downtown too late into the evening. Although there were still times when I stopped in after work and visited.

As part of Mother's care, I was required to attend monthly meetings with the staff to evaluate Mom's care and progress, if any. I knew that Carol would have questions and want to be a part of these monthly conferences. In order to accommodate this, I drove to SMH to attend the conference in person and then conferenced Carol in by phone. This was perfect for me. Carol could get all the information firsthand without relying on me to pass it on. The conferences didn't last long. Essentially, the floor nurses reported on how it was going with Mom. The activities director would let us know if Mom was participating in any of the offerings. We would get a report on the food she was eating (or not). We also received a report from the administration office regarding her financial report. Because of Medicaid restrictions, she was only allowed to have $1,500 max in her account at any given time.

No surprise to us, most of the reports told us she wasn't eating that much, she wasn't participating in any of the activities or groups, and she didn't like to take baths. Fortunately for us, she had no choice. The nurses made her take a bath. She was no longer allowed to sit in her own stink. Debbie was also at the meeting and wondered if Mother would benefit from a psychiatric evaluation and possibly some antidepressants. Apparently, I wasn't the only one suffering from Mother's foul moods. After the conference, I called Carol to talk to her privately. We discussed the antidepressant idea and agreed it might help. We had thought for some time that Mom could benefit from medication, but I hesitated going down that road since she was not reliably taking any of her medications. If she didn't take the antidepressants on a daily basis, they weren't going to help her much. Now that the nursing home would be taking the responsibility, it might work. Carol and I also made the decision to sign Mom up for weekly hair appointments. The nursing home had its own little hair salon next to the dining room. At least, Mom could have her hair washed and set once a week, which would also help with the smell, and it would be an opportunity to draw down her money a little at a time. Even though the nursing home was using most of her Social Security income to house her, she was still allowed to have some of her monthly income. The administration office kept track of her balance so she wouldn't go over the limit.

During another one of the conferences, I learned she was nearing the maximum amount of money she was allowed, and I needed to spend down her account. The finance director, Emily, suggested I spend the account down to around $1,000 so that the balance wouldn't build back up so quickly. Now, I had to decide how to spend $500 on someone who didn't need anything. Unfortunately, I couldn't just give the money away. It had to be spent for Mother's benefit. Emily then offered some suggestions for using the money.

Taking all the suggestions into consideration, I decided to spend my next Saturday taking Mother shopping. At least, she would have a great time. I arrived during lunch. I really didn't want to take her out to eat, so I found her in the dining room and sat with her while she picked at her food.

"I thought I would take you out shopping for a little while this afternoon. What do you think?"

"I guess that would be okay." I don't know why I was expecting a little more excitement at this.

"Great. As soon as you finish your lunch, we'll be on our way."

"I guess we can go now."

"You didn't eat very much. Can you eat a few more bites?"

"It doesn't taste that good. The food here is bland."

"Did you try some salt and pepper on it?"

"I'm not allowed to have salt. It's not good for my blood pressure."

"Um, there is a salt shaker sitting right here. If you weren't allowed to have salt, they would not put a shaker on your table."

"They didn't tell me I couldn't have it. I just watch what I eat and don't add salt."

Being pretty sure my head was about to explode, I said, "Don't you want to stay for dessert? Looks like they are handing out ice cream."

When the server reached her table, we found it wasn't ice cream but pudding.

"I can just take it to my room and eat it later after we get back."

"Oh. You're allowed to take food to your room?"

"Sure. They pick up the empty dishes later."

"Wow. It's kind of like being in a hotel," I quipped.

"No. It's not." The joke fell flat.

I took Mom to a mall near where she lived. I really did not want to walk the entire mall, so I picked a department store that handled all kinds of merchandise.

"I thought we would buy you some new clothes. Winter will be here in a couple of months, so we can get you some warmer clothes."

"Okay."

The door I chose to enter opened into the shoe department. (They really should put a sign out front warning people.) Needless to say, we didn't make it any farther.

"I could use a new pair of shoes."

"Of course, you could. Do you want to get a pair of walking shoes?"

"What do I need walking shoes for? I never walk anywhere."

"Right."

"These are cute. Can we see if they have my size?"

"You already have a pair that look very similar to these."

"But these are brown. My other pair is black."

"How silly of me."

A half hour later, she had settled on the shoes in the size and color she wanted. Why fight it? We were there to spend money, and the shoes were for her. I'm sure the government didn't care if she bought a pair of shoes exactly like a pair she already had to sit unworn in her closet.

From there, we made it all the way to the women's department. We walked every square inch. I pointed out things I thought looked good. She turned her nose up at all of them. Finally, she told me just to pick out some things as she couldn't decide. I put together about five outfits. At least she would look good going to the hairdresser and the dining hall.

"I could use some new underwear. The elastic is all out of mine."

"Great. We can do that." We made our way to the lingerie department. Once there, she got a second wind.

"Oh, I could use some new pajamas too."

"Would you rather have a nightgown?"

"No. I like pajamas."

I was thinking nightgowns would probably be easier for the nursing staff, but there was no way I was going to rock this boat again. We added a couple pairs of pajamas to our purchases and left the store. I had managed to spend $600 on Mother in a couple of hours. Who knew it would be so easy?

On my way home, I called Carol (hands-free) to give her a report on the day's events. She told me she had called Mom the day before, and she was not in a very good mood. She told Carol she wanted to "get the hell out of here" (here being SMH). She even threatened to get a lawyer.

"I'll see what I can do. If I have to strong-arm it, I will. This is no place for a human being. I'm sick of this place. It is going to hit the fan soon. The four walls cave in on you some days."

Once she got that out of her system, she changed the subject to the roses in the garden. Carol and I marveled at how fast she was able to shift gears. Once the subject of the roses and the garden surfaced, there was no more talk of lawyers or leaving. Some days, our heads just spin.

THIRTY-FIVE

Because Mother was a Medicaid resident at the nursing home, she could not be away from SMH for any extended length of time. For instance, if she needed to go to the hospital for any reason and she would be there longer than three days, she would lose her room, and we would have to start the process all over again. She could be away overnight or for a few hours, but that was the extent of it. Not wanting to risk an argument about not wanting to go back, I limited her "off-site" visits to short shopping trips or eating out. By Thanksgiving, she hadn't been out anywhere significant since she moved in the prior March. I thought it might be nice for her to come for Thanksgiving dinner. My daughter had an apartment within a few miles of SMH, so we agreed she would bring Grandma to dinner and then I would take her back afterward. My son would be at my house with his family, and this would give Mom an opportunity to see her great-granddaughter and spend some time with her grandchildren and family. I often forgot that these were not my mother's favorite things to do, but I persisted. These were my very favorite things to do. I never passed up an opportunity to see my grandchild or my children. Therefore, I asked Lynn to pick her up before noon so she could have more of a day "out."

Although I had called Mom to let her know the arrangements, she didn't remember any of it. Lynn arrived in her room around 11:00 a.m. that day.

"Hi, Grandma!"

"What are you doing here?"

Ignoring the sour reception, Lynn continued, "I'm here to take you to Mom's for Thanksgiving."

"It's Thanksgiving?"

"It sure is. Jimmy, Rachel, and Hannah will be there too."

"Who are they?"

"Jimmy is your grandson?" (Pause) "Rachel is his wife?" (Pause) "Hannah is your great-granddaughter?"

"Jimmy's married?"

"Yes. For three years now."

"Oh. When did that happen?"

"Three years ago, in 2005."

"Did I know about that?"

"Yes, you did."

"Humpf. Well, we can't go yet."

"Why not?

"The parade isn't over. I'm watching the parade. I always watch the parade."

"Well, Mom wanted us to be early to her house."

"We will go as soon as the parade is over."

"Since you are watching the parade, I'm going to go down to the nurses' station and say hello to Theresa." As Lynn stepped out into the hall, she dialed my phone number.

"Mom."

"Hi, sweetie, are you on your way?"

"Mom. She won't leave. She's watching the parade and says she won't leave until it's over."

"Oh, brother. Well, there isn't much we can do about it. If you force her to leave, she will be in an even worse mood for the rest of the day. It's okay. We will just see you when you get here."

"I'll text you when we are on the way."

"Okay. Be careful. Try to stay positive."

"Yeah. Right."

Arriving well after noon, Mother made her displeasure known immediately. Jimmy and Rachel greeted her, and Jimmy tried to hug her.

She just stared at Hannah as if she were a space alien. At three years of age, Hannah was the smartest of all. She stayed as far away from Grandma as she could.

As I was dishing up the food and setting it on the table, Mother said to me, "Am I going to get back in time for dinner?"

"Mom, you are having dinner here. It's Thanksgiving. I thought you would enjoy having Thanksgiving with your family." Before she could make any other snide remark, I asked, "How was the parade?"

"It was okay. There are just too many commercials. You don't even get to see much of the parade itself."

"Did you get to see Santa?"

"Yep. He always brings up the rear."

"I know. That's Macy's way of saying Thanksgiving is over and it's time for Christmas shopping." We all chuckled, but Mom didn't understand.

Somehow, we managed to salvage the day and enjoy our time together. Lynn left to stop by her boyfriend's house, and I told Mom I would take her home. Kindly, Jimmy and Rachel volunteered to go with me. At least, I didn't have to endure the ride alone. At the nursing home, Mother provided the tour of the facility (i.e., fish, birds, dining hall, etc.) ending with her room and the view out her room. Jimmy and Rachel kindly commented on what a nice place it was. I thought for sure that would produce a rise from her, but she just nodded graciously. (Just when I thought I had her figured out.) As we prepared to leave, she wanted to give Hannah a hug. Hannah was pretty sure she didn't want to do that, but she timidly agreed. She didn't hug for long, but she did make the gesture. Little did we know at the time that would be the last time they saw Grandma. I was thankful the day had gone so well, despite the initial bumps.

Since Mom was neither grateful nor excited about coming to my house for Thanksgiving, I decided I wasn't going to go through that again for Christmas. Thanksgiving is the big holiday at my house. Christmas is more laidback. My son and his family live three and half hours away, so we never see them on Christmas Day. We had a quiet meal with my daughter and her boyfriend, and then I drove to Cincinnati after dinner. I arrived in Mother's room while she was watching a movie, laden with a few of her favorite things. I bought her a box of Esther Price, her favorite chocolates, and a tin of Christmas cookies. She seemed happy enough with the gifts, and we actually had a pleasant visit. I commented about the wreath on her door and how nice it looked. The nursing home had told me earlier that they did not allow Christmas trees in the residents' rooms—too much of a risk. So I purchased a wreath for Mom's door instead. At least, it added a little Christmas spirit to the room. Thankfully, she never asked about a Christmas tree and why she didn't have one. I think by that time she figured, they were too much trouble anyway.

On the drive home, I decided this was the way holidays would be handled in the future. Mom did not appear to care one way or the other. All the days were the same to her. I needed to give myself a break and quit trying to force my wishes upon her. Just because I loved being with my family, I did not need to force her into that situation. Just because the holidays were special to me, didn't mean that she needed to feel the same way. I had to try to let the guilt feelings go. Because of guilt, I was trying to force Mother into a life she didn't want. Perhaps, I would feel less guilty if I just let her be who she was.

THIRTY-SIX

On February 8, 2009, mother turned ninety years of age. You know me by now. I thought I should try to make it a special event for Mom. Not everyone gets a ninetieth birthday. She was one of the lucky few. I told the staff I wanted to do something for her special day. They told me I could have a little party for her in the activity room at the end of the hall. As it turned out, her birthday fell on a Sunday that year. I've been known to make special occasion cakes for family and friends, so I made a decorated cake for Mom. I picked up an arrangement of flowers at the grocery. My daughter picked up a couple of balloons. Last, but no means least, I arranged a surprise visit from her brother. They hadn't seen each other in over a year, and, silly me, I thought she would enjoy it. Uncle Ray said he would drive to Lebanon, and then I could drive the rest of the way to Cincinnati. It was so good to see him and Aunt Charlotte as I hadn't seen them in quite a while either. We talked all the way to Cincinnati. A drive with Uncle Ray was much different from a drive with his sister, believe me.

We all walked into the nursing home carrying something for Mom's party. We carried all our things past Mother's room to the activity room down the hall. Lynn tied the balloons on some of the chairs. I took the cake out of the box and displayed it with the flowers on one of the tables. I had Aunt Charlotte and Uncle Ray take a seat and left Ben with them while I went to get Mother. She hadn't even noticed us walk past her room. I entered her room. She was just sitting in her chair staring into space.

"Happy birthday!" I greeted her.

"Oh, hi. Someone that looked almost like you just walked down the hall a little while ago."

"Really? I think that might have been me." I smiled.

"What are you doing here?"

"Well, I came to celebrate your birthday with you."

"Who said it was my birthday?"

"I think I know when your birthday is. I've known you all my life. You're ninety years old today!"

"I can't be that old."

"I know it probably doesn't seem like it, but you definitely are. Let's go down the hall."

"What for?"

"There is something down there I want to show you."

"Oh, all right."

We walked down the hall, and I entered the room first. Mother entered and looked around. "You did all this for me?"

"Of course."

"I don't know what all the fuss is about. It's just a birthday."

"But it's your ninetieth birthday. I wanted it to be special. Did you see who is here?"

"Yeah, I saw."

"It's Uncle Ray and Aunt Charlotte."

"I know who they are."

"Don't you want to say hello at least?"

"Hello."

I was shocked. I know you are probably saying "why" right about now. Here was her own brother whom she hadn't seen in over a year, and she couldn't think of one thing to say to him. Leaden silence filled the room. Even I was speechless. Thank God for my daughter who finally broke the ice.

"Grandma, did you see the cake Mom made for you?"

She looked at me. "You made that?"

"Yes."

"Huh. I thought you got it at the store."

"No. I made it. I also picked out the flowers. I bought flowers that would bloom for a few weeks so you can enjoy them in your room. Would you like to have a piece of cake?"

"Can I go invite Chris to join us?"

"Sure. There's plenty to go around."

She left the room, and I explained to the group that Chris was the man who lived across the hall from Mom. They had struck up a friendship. Go figure. An eligible bachelor moved in. Of course, Mother was going to make friends. Mother always did love men. That was one of her biggest problems over her lifetime. She liked them whether they were available or not!

Returning with Chris, we all gathered around the table and sang happy birthday. I cut the cake, and Lynn poured coffee. The nursing home offered to provide drinks for our little party. After finishing his cake, Chris excused himself. Soon after that, I said I needed to get Aunt Charlotte and Uncle Ray back to Lebanon so they wouldn't have to drive home in the dark. We carried Mother's flowers and balloons back to her room and said our goodbyes. I dropped the leftover cake at the nurses' station for the staff to enjoy. Once in the car, I profusely apologized to Aunt Charlotte and Uncle Ray.

"I am so sorry. I had no idea she would react that way."

"It's okay. Don't worry about it. Nothing your mother does surprises me," said Uncle Ray.

"Still. Even for her, I never guessed she would be so rude. I so appreciate your making the effort to come. I enjoyed having you even if she didn't."

"No problem, Diane. Really."

Back in Lebanon, I hugged them goodbye and told them I loved them. They told me they loved me. I didn't know that would be the last time I saw my uncle Ray.

THIRTY-SEVEN

In July of 2009, Carol and Pete returned to Ohio for the occasion of my daughter's wedding. My daughter was marrying a man that I felt did not "fit." I was not the happy mother of the bride I should have been, but I was trying to make it the special day my daughter wanted. My sister decided I needed the moral support and made the long trip to Ohio. I was hosting the rehearsal dinner because the groom's parents were not in a position to do so. Carol and Pete helped me prep food. They helped me at the church the next day and got me through the reception. She really had been my support, just like she had been through all my life.

The very best plan of the wedding was not inviting my mother. My sister and I felt I had enough on my plate without worrying about what Mother was doing. Besides that, I would have to leave the party early to get her back to the nursing home. I'd be spending most of the night on the road. It was just better if Mom stayed, oblivious as to what was happening around her. Why add more stress to an already boiling pot of stress?

After the wedding was over, the cleanup done, and the unhappy couple on their way to their honeymoon, we decided to visit Mother. Since she didn't know anything about the wedding and had no idea Carol and Pete were in town, we thought we would just spring it on her. We arrived at SMH at dinnertime. I went to Mom's room while Carol and Pete waited outside the dining hall. Mom and I disembarked from the elevator to see two people sitting on the bench where Mom usually waited for the dining room to open. She smiled and acknowledged the two strangers. She and I sat down on the bench next to them. Carol spoke to Mom, but Mom had no clue who she was. Pete got up and walked over to one of the pictures on the wall. Mom kept looking at him quizzically. "What's wrong, Mom?"

"That man."

"What about that man?"

"He looks just like my son-in-law from Alaska."

"Maybe that's because he is your son-in-law from Alaska."

Her eyes grew big as she asked, "Really?"

"Really."

"Where's Carol? Did she come with him?"

My sister responded, "I'm sitting right here, Mother."

Mom turned toward Carol. "Well, where did you come from?"

"I've been sitting here ever since you got off the elevator. You looked right at me and even spoke to me." While we all had a good laugh and chatted, I felt uneasy. It seemed to me the dementia was getting worse. She didn't even recognize her own daughter anymore. How much longer would it be before she no longer recognized me? Granted, she saw me every week, but did she really know how I was? I had to ask.

"Mom, do you know who I am?"

"You're Diane. Of course, I know who you are. Why are you being so silly?"

I just shrugged and smiled, still not convinced she knew exactly who I was. She knew I was Diane, but did she know who Diane was in relation to herself? I didn't take it any further. The visit was going pretty well, and I didn't want to throw a wet blanket on it. Still. It was a very unsettling visit.

Once back in Alaska, I continued weekly communication with my sister regarding Mom. Most times, I also included my nieces (Carol's children) and my daughter. I regaled my family with weekly emails detailing my visits with Mother. Humor was a coping mechanism for keeping sane. Sarcasm was another, in case you hadn't figure that out yet. She was such an easy mark. The dementia kept her so far on the outer fringes that she never understood when you were laughing at her or making a joke at her expense. I didn't say this to be mean. I never felt I was being mean to Mother. But when I relayed information to my family, it was just so much easier to make it seem as innocuous as possible. All of them lived too far away to fully understand the magnitude of the situation. Why burden them? This way, Grandma was hysterical, instead of brash and rude. Deep down, they knew the truth. Humor made it easier for all of us.

One of my sister's emails asked how the visit with Mother went the prior week. In response, I wrote the following long email:

> In short, it was a disaster. I arrived with a bouquet of flowers and that seemed to bring a smile. I asked her if she would like to go out to eat, and she was agreeable. Then the bottom fell out. As we were leaving, she turned to me and asked if she was ever going to be moving from that place. I told her no, that this is where she lives now. She said, "I don't like that. People come and go from here all the time." I had to bite my tongue to keep from saying that the only way people leave there is in a box, but I managed. From that point on, she pouted and cried the entire visit. I took her to Boston Market for dinner. She only ate a few bites and cried all through dinner. I then took her shoe shopping, and we found a nice pair of loafer-type shoes that seemed to cheer her for a brief moment, and then it was back to pouting. I took her back to SMH, dropped her at her room, tried to hug her (nothing), and told her I'd be back soon. She just turned away. Great visit.

Unfortunately, glutton for punishment that I am, I went to see her again last night. Lynn met me there after work, and we went in together (for strength). The elevator landed on the third floor, the doors opened, and there stood Mother with the most hateful look on her face you can imagine. I cheerfully said hello, trying to change her mood, which didn't work. I told her we came for a visit. Nothing. Still the hateful look.

I said, "Gee, don't be so glad to see us."

Her reply was, "Why should I?" Still shooting daggers from her eyes.

I looked her in the eye and said, "If you want me to leave, I will. I don't want to impose myself on you. If this is not a good time for you, I will come some other time. Just tell me, and I will leave."

Now, mind you, all this conversation was happening while Lynn and I were standing in the elevator and Mother was standing in the hall in front of the busy nurses' station. I knew they had to have heard the exchange. She finally said she was heading down to the dining hall. I said we would go with her. When we got to the ground level, her man friend in the wheelchair was sitting there. Of course, Lynn knew him, and he recognized Lynn, so they exchanged pleasantries while Mother looked on. We sat on the bench for a few minutes, then she was curious about the picture on the wall showing the riverfront of Cincinnati in 1948 versus 1988. We talked about the picture for a while. I showed her my office building and where I parked. We talked about all that had changed over the years—at least it eased the tension. Then she asked if we'd seen the birds. I said, "Not yet today." So we walked down and watched the birds, which seemed to cheer her a little. Then we went outside and sat in the courtyard for what felt like a year until it was time for her to got to the dining room. We dropped her off there, and she had the disgusted look again. I told her I would call her the next time before I came to make sure she was up to visitors, and we left.

Two weeks in a row of bad behavior was just too much. I kept asking God what I was supposed to be learning from this. I could only imagine what it must be like to have to live in those confines. I would like to think, though, if I were in a similar situation, I would try to make the most of it. I don't know. As nursing homes go, I think SMH offers much to its residents.

When we were in the hall with the birds, a lady named Anne, who Lynn also knew and whom Mother always speaks to whenever we run into her, spoke to Mom. She was such a pleasant person. I knew she must not like the fact that she had to be there either, but she was trying to make the most of it. She always dressed nice. She wore makeup. Her hair was always done. You could just tell that she was a content individual. I so wished mother could be as content, but I didn't believe she had ever known that state of mind in her entire life.

If I'm learning anything from this, it's to keep a positive mindset no matter what. I fall victim every now and then to depression, but so far, nothing that keeps me down for very long. I am striving to keep this frame of mind in my new job as well as life in general.

THIRTY-EIGHT

In October of 2010, Ben and I were married in a small family ceremony on our patio. We decided on a quiet event with just our kids and my lifelong best friend. The day was absolutely gorgeous, and we had a wonderful time. Mother was not invited. She didn't even know we were planning to get married. For all I knew, she probably thought we were already married. We had been together for thirteen years. He had been around ever since she moved to Ohio from Florida. She never asked, and I never brought it up. So when I went SMH the following week, I decided to test the water.

"Ben and I got married last weekend."

"Huh." (Pause) "Are we going out to dinner?"

"Did you hear what I said?"

"I heard you. What's the big deal?"

"No big deal. Let's go to dinner."

And that's all there was to that. I could have just as easily told her I cut my arm off and gotten the same reaction.

A week after Thanksgiving that year, I had stopped at Sam's Club on my way home from work. I had just finished loading a couple of hundred dollars' worth of groceries in my trunk when my phone rang. I pulled it out of my purse and answered.

"Is this Diane?"

"Yes."

"Hi, Diane. This is Theresa at St. Margaret Hall."

"Oh, hi."

"I'm calling to let you know that your mom is being taken to Jewish Hospital. The ambulance is on the way.

I know you live pretty far away, so it will probably be easier for you to meet her at the hospital emergency room."

"What in the world happened? Is she okay?"

"She's okay, but we think she broke her hip. She was standing at the elevator in front of the nurses' station waiting to go down for dinner. One minute she was standing there, the next minute she was on the floor. We assessed the situation, called her doctor, and called for the ambulance. Jewish Hospital is where we send any resident who needs hospital care."

"Oh, wow. Okay. I just loaded my car with groceries. I am going to take those home and then will be on my way to the hospital."

"That's no problem at all. The ambulance isn't even here yet, so you will probably end up at the hospital at the same time."

"Thank you for calling."

I called Ben from the car to let him know what was happening. He met me in the driveway to help unload the car. We stowed the perishables in the refrigerator and left everything else sitting on the kitchen table. On the drive to Cincinnati, I called my sister (hands-free) to fill her in. Thankfully, the Interstate traffic had died down since rush hour, and we made good time.

Upon entering the ER, I asked for my mom. A nurse showed me to the temporary cubicle where she was lying on a gurney. She was lying on her left side with her back to the entrance of the cubicle. I made my way around to face her.

"How are you feeling?"

"I feel okay. My hip hurts really bad."

"I know. Theresa at SMH called me. Has the ER doctor taken an x-ray or anything?"

"Not yet."

"Have they given you anything for the pain?"

"I don't think so."

"Has your pain level changed at all since you've been here?"

"I don't know."

Feeling frustrated with the answers, or lack thereof, a nurse rounded the curtain.

"Are you Mrs. Adams?"

"No. Mrs. Zella. Diane Zella. I'm Ethel's daughter."

"Oh. I thought they told me your name was Adams."

"I remarried a couple of months ago."

"Well, congratulations."

"Thanks."

"I just wanted to let you know we are getting ready to take your mom to x-ray. You are welcome to sit here and wait, or you can return to the waiting room where the chairs are a bit more comfortable."

"That's okay. We'll stay here."

"That's fine. An orderly will be in any minute."

"Thanks. Oh, can you tell me…has she had any pain medication?"

"The nursing home staff gave her a little something, but the doctor wants to wait until we see what we are dealing with."

"I understand, but she seems to be in significant pain."

"I know. We will get a handle on that just as soon as possible."

"Thank you."

The nurse left, and I turned to Mom.

"Did you hear what the nurse said?"

"Yes."

"Are you wearing any jewelry? If so, we need to take that off before you go to x-ray. We don't want to lose it."

"I have this ring on, and I have some earrings in."

"Okay. Can you get the ring off?"

"It's a little tight, but I think I can."

Mother handed me her ring. I smiled as I put it on my finger for safekeeping. It was the mother's ring I had bought her years before for Mother's Day. She then tried to get her earrings out but was struggling. "Here, let me try. When was the last time you changed your earrings?"

"It's been a while."

"I guess so. They are a little crusty." I wrapped the earrings in a tissue and put them in my purse.

Just about that time, the orderly came in to take her to x-ray. I kissed her forehead and told her we would be waiting right there when she finished. The orderly wheeled her down the hallway, and I began to cry. Suddenly, she looked so frail and fragile. I couldn't help thinking about a broken hip and what that would mean for her life. I had always heard that elderly people rarely recovered from a broken hip. But this was my mom. She was going to be just fine. After all, look how tough she was and had been all her life. It's going to take more than a broken hip to bring her down.

Ben and I quietly chatted while waiting for Mother to return. A doctor appeared before Mother came back.

"The nursing home was correct. She has a broken hip. Frankly, I don't know how she has been moving up until now. There is very little there at all. The socket is completely crumbled. This could have happened months ago."

"Wow. So what do we do now?"

"She will have to have a hip replacement."

"At her age?"

"There really is nothing else we can do. She doesn't have enough bone left to try to pin it. It will have to be replaced."

"Can she survive the anesthesia?"

"Well, that is a concern. She seems to be in relatively good health otherwise. The thing is, if we don't replace the hip, she will be completely bedridden and in pain. If we do the surgery and she comes through the anesthesia, she will be walking again. Of course, there will be physical therapy, but she should be in good shape."

"I don't want to see her bedridden. That's for sure. And I don't want her to be in pain. So how soon can we have the surgery done?

"Tomorrow."

"Tomorrow?"

"Yes, I have her on the schedule for 10:00 a.m. Right now, they are getting a room ready for her. They should be bringing her back here until the room is finished. We will keep her pretty medicated overnight to ease the pain."

"That is great news. We will wait here with her until she gets to her room. Thank you for everything, Doctor."

"You're welcome. Will you be here tomorrow for the surgery?"

"Yes."

"Then, I'll see you tomorrow."

"Thanks again."

As promised, Ben and I waited for Mother to be transferred to her room. I tried to talk to her and tell her I'd be back in the morning, but the medications had already taken effect, and she was too groggy to understand. On the drive home, Ben asked, "What about work? Will they let you off?"

"Well, while Jay might not be happy about it, it's not up to her. I'm going directly to Human Resources. I know they will have no problem with it."

"That's good. At least, you have someone higher up who will do the right thing."

Early the next morning, I went into the office as normal and went directly to HR. I explained the situation and was told to take as much time as I needed. I then went to tell my boss the plan. I was taking my laptop with me and working from the hospital. The hospital had free Wi-Fi and with remote credentials; I could access the office network as if I were sitting at my desk. I planned to work from the hospital the following day as well until Mom was released back to the nursing home. Because she was in a nursing facility, the hospital stay did not need to be long. This was even better news. I did not want Mom to lose her room and have to go through trying to get it back. My boss said she would see me in two days.

I arrived at Mom's hospital room as the anesthesiologist was beginning preparations. I kissed Mom's forehead and told her I would be here when she woke up. Sitting in the waiting room, I was thankful to have work to keep my mind occupied. The time went by quickly, and I accomplished much. Before I knew it, the doctor was coming through the door to brief me.

"Your mom did very well. She is in recovery now and will probably be there for another hour if you want to get something to eat or drink."

"How does the hip look?"

"Perfect. The surgery went well. We found enough bone for attaching the new joint. She is going to be good as new."

"Only if you gave her a new brain while she was under." I laughed.

The doctor chuckled. "No. Afraid not. She still has her brain."

"Thank you, Doctor, I really appreciate your being able to get this done so quickly."

"No problem. You have a good day now."

"Thank you. You too."

Relieved, I returned to my chair and my computer. I had everyone I knew praying for Mom, so I needed to update them about her surgery and prognosis. Soon, the nurse came to take me to Mom's room. Apparently, she was awake and wanting something to eat. That sounded about right.

As I walked through her room door, the nurse was getting her out of bed to go to the bathroom. Shocked, I asked, "You're getting her out of bed already?"

"We want them up and moving as soon as possible. She has to have help, and we don't want her full weight on the right hip, but we also don't want her muscles to atrophy any faster."

"I'm glad you're in charge of moving her and not me."

The nurse smiled. "That's what I get paid for!"

I sat with Mom as she dozed off and on throughout the evening. There was a couch/bed in her room where the nursing staff had told me I could sleep if I wanted to spend the night. Once Mom appeared to be down for the count, I laid down and fell asleep. Actually, I slept quite well. I couldn't believe it. I guess I was just exhausted enough that my body didn't fight it. When they brought Mom's breakfast tray, they also brought one for me. Coffee was the most important thing, but I did manage to eat most of the food they brought me. I worked the rest of the day from the couch while also talking with Mom and trying to keep her spirits up. The ambulance staff arrived around 3:00 p.m. to return her to SMH. At that time, I told her goodbye and that I would come to see her the next day. I texted Ben that I was on my way home.

My husband is so good to me. He fixed dinner for me that night. After my shower, I just collapsed into bed. What a week it had been!

THIRTY-NINE

The doctor had been partially correct. Over the course of the next couple of weeks, Mother made vast improvements. I went to visit a couple of times a week. On one visit, I arrived on the third floor to see her walking down the hallway, holding onto a grab bar, with a nurse at her side. The nurse wasn't holding onto her. She was walking under her own power. When she turned to walk back to her room, she saw me standing in the doorway.

"Look at you! Great job!"

"Yeah, she makes me walk down the hall all day long."

"Well, you want to be able to walk by yourself again, don't you?"

"I guess. They gave me a wheelchair. Why can't I just use that?"

"Believe me, you do not want to have to use a wheelchair to get around. Do you remember my friend, Sharon?"

"I remember Sharon."

"She was in a wheelchair for three years before she died. It's a lot of hard work."

"I still think it would be easier."

"Does it hurt when you walk?"

"No."

"Then why don't you want to walk?"

"I get tired too easily and get out of breath."

"That's another reason to keep it up. You need to build up your strength again."

When we got into Mom's room, the nurse helped her into the wheelchair, and I noticed Mom's recliner was gone.

"What happened to Mom's chair?"

"We had it moved to the basement storage for a while. We don't want your mom sitting with her legs crossed or raised up. She shouldn't put too much pressure on that hip for another couple of weeks. She is doing well with her physical therapy, but we still need to be careful."

"Oh. I didn't know."

"We want her to sit in the wheelchair. We have this little device in place so she won't cross her legs. We noticed she tends to sit with her legs crossed, and that isn't good for her right now. If you see her try to cross her legs, gently remind her."

"I'll be sure to do that. Thank you for letting me know."

After Mom settled in the wheelchair, she didn't seem to want to talk anymore. I tried asking her what she'd like to have for Christmas. I tried to get her to converse about anything. After twenty minutes, I'd had enough and left to get back to the office. I was on my lunch hour.

A couple of weeks after the surgery, we had our monthly conference with the staff. The nurses reported that Mom was not eating or drinking. They were also having a difficult time getting her to leave the wheelchair. She had been cleared by physical therapy to walk without assistance, but she just wouldn't do it. Because she was not getting proper nutrition, they were going to start her on protein shakes. The nurses told me I could bring food in from her favorite restaurant if I wanted. Anything to try to get her to eat. Although the surgery had been successful, as far as her body was concerned, her mind seemed to be suffering more than ever. She was talking less. She didn't want to go to the dining room for meals anymore, so they were bringing trays to her in her room. However, she didn't touch the food, not even the dessert.

At the sound of this, I was very concerned. After the conference was over, I went to Mom's room. She was sitting in front of the television in the wheelchair.

"Would you like to take a walk and visit the birds?" I asked.

"No."

"How about if we take the elevator down to the second floor and check in on the fish?"

"No."

"Mom, we need to get you out of that wheelchair. How about a short walk down to the activity room?"

"I'm fine right here."

At that point, one of the nurses came in with a can of protein shake and a glass.

"Ethel, I have a nice strawberry shake here for you. I'm going to set it right here on your tray. Try to drink some, okay?"

Mother looked from the nurse to the shake and said nothing.

Helplessly, I looked at the nurse and said, "I'll be here for another few minutes. I'll see if I can get her to drink any of it."

"Thanks. Don't force her, but see if you can get any of it down."

"I will."

The nurse left, and I talked to Mom for a few minutes about whatever was on the television. I couldn't get her to respond at all. I picked up the shake and handed it to her, coaxing her to drink a little. She took the glass from me and set it back on the tray. Near tears, I told her I needed to get back to the office and encouraged her to try to drink the shake. I couldn't hold the tears in any longer and sat in the parking lot crying. I needed to pull it together before returning to work.

I continued to visit Mom every couple of days, but she did not improve. Each time, I found her sitting in the wheelchair in front of the television. Now, though, she wasn't even watching the television. She just sat there staring blankly. She was unresponsive to any conversation I tried. The nurses told me she was drinking a little of the shakes but not enough to do any good. They were not having any luck getting her to drink water either, and she was becoming dehydrated. If they couldn't get her to drink, they would have to put her on an IV.

A couple of days before Christmas, I visited with some "goodies" for her, hoping I could entice her to eat some of her favorite things. I brought her a big tin of Danish sugar cookies, a giant Hershey bar with almonds, and a box of Esther Price chocolate. I had also gone through the drive-through at Wendy's and picked up a Frosty for her. As I handed each item to her, she looked at it and then put it on her tray. The chocolate and cookies hadn't worked, maybe the Frosty? I handed that to her, and she seemed to perk up for a minute. She actually took a couple of bites, but then set it on her tray.

"You'd better eat that before it melts."

"I'll eat it later."

Words! She actually spoke words.

"Later, it will be soup, and you'll have to drink it." A little smile curled at the corners of her mouth, but she didn't say anything else. After a tortuous hour, I couldn't take anymore. I kissed her goodbye and told her I loved her.

"I'll see if I can get down sometime on Christmas Day." No acknowledgment.

On the drive home, I wondered why I thought I'd go for a visit on Christmas Day. She didn't know when Christmas Day was. She also wouldn't know whether I had been there on that specific day. When Christmas Day arrived, I had talked myself into not going to Cincinnati. In fact, I waited until a few days after Christmas before visiting Mother again. The next time I visited, the nurses were watching for me. "Mrs. Zella, before you go to your mom's room, we need to talk to you."

"Okay."

"We have not been able to get her to eat or drink since your last visit, so we've had to put her on an IV to get some kind of nutrition into her body. We hope it will only be temporary, but we wanted to tell you before you see her."

"When did this happen?"

"About an hour ago. We were just about to call you."

"Okay. Do you really think this is only going to be temporary? She doesn't talk to me at all when I come to visit now. Frankly, I'm not even sure if she recognizes me or knows who I am."

"We can't know for certain. We hope this will only be temporary, but we can't promise you that."

"I understand."

With that information, I felt as if I were wearing lead shoes as I walked toward Mother's door. She was lying in bed looking at the needle in her arm. She took her other hand and reached for the needle.

"No! Mom, you need to leave that alone."

She looked at me without seeing me and reached again for the needle. I pushed the call button next to her bed, and a nurse arrived almost immediately.

"She acts like she is trying to pull the needle out of her arm."

The nurse gently checked the needle and told Mom that the needle had to stay in her arm. She added another strip of tape, hoping that would deter Mom. I sat on the edge of the bed holding her hand, trying to distract her. That worked for a short time, and then she was at it again.

"Mom, if you pull that out, it is going to hurt really bad, and you will start bleeding. You need to not touch it. Do you understand?"

She just looked at me, but she didn't reach for the needle again. I began to ramble on about all kinds of nonsensical things, trying to keep her attention on me and not her arm. I was able to keep her occupied until I had to leave. On my way out, I stopped at the nurses' station to let them know she was still trying to get the needle out. They indicated they would handle it.

The first week of January, I visited Mom every other day. The only change was her sleeping constantly. The nursing staff had resorted to a sedative to keep the IV in her arm. Apparently, after I'd left a couple of days before, she successfully pulled the needle out of her arm. The only way to keep it in was to "partially" sedate her. To me, it didn't seem partial. She appeared to be out completely. My favorite nurse, Theresa, stopped by Mom's room while I was there.

"Mrs. Zella," she said quietly, "you should know that your mom has reached the end stage of life. Her body is barely functioning. We keep the IV and the sedation in place to make her comfortable, but there is nothing else we can do for her. I reviewed her file and saw that you signed a "do not resuscitate" (DNR) order when she was admitted."

"Yes, that's correct."

"She could potentially 'live' like this for days or weeks. I've seen patients live quite a while without eating or drinking anything. I also noticed in her Health Care Power she did not agree to 'pulling the plug.'"

"My sister and I, both, tried to get her to change her mind on that, but she was adamant. We will just have to watch her in this state until she decides she's had enough."

"I'm so sorry. I know how hard that is for you and your sister."

"I don't really know what she thought she would gain by remaining in this state, but it's too late now. Thank you for taking such good care of her while she's been here," I said as I stifled a sob. "Hopefully, it won't be much longer."

"I hope so too. Of course, we will call you the minute anything changes."

"Thank you. I'll still continue to stop by."

With that, I left the nursing home and cried all the way home. Seeing her lying in bed, she looked so small and fragile. I had never seen my mother look fragile in her life. She was always strong and defiant.

I didn't go to the nursing home over the weekend but did stop in on my lunch hour on Monday, January 10. I sat on the side of Mom's bed talking to her as if she could understand me. After about fifteen minutes, I headed back to work.

On Tuesday, the weather was turning icy, so I left work early to try to get home before rush hour and dark. As usual, I walked in the door and started on dinner. While the food was cooking, I changed into comfortable clothes. Ben and I sat down to eat, and my phone rang. The nursing home was calling. I laid my fork down.

"Hello?"

"Hello, Diane? This is Theresa from SMH. I wanted to let you know that your mother is fading. Her blood pressure is low as is her breathing. I really don't think it will be much longer. I know you wanted to see her again before she died. You should probably come now."

I looked at the clock. It was 6:45 p.m. "Okay. We are just finishing with dinner, and we will be on our way. I think we can be there by seven thirty. Do you think she will last that long?"

"Oh, yes. I think she still has a few hours. You'll be fine."

Ben and I gulped the last few bites and grabbed our coats. Walking out the front door, the snow was beginning to fall a little heavier. Hopefully, the salt trucks would be out and the Interstate would be clear. We arrived at SMH around 7:40 p.m. Ben sat in Mom's rocking chair, and I sat on the edge of her bed. What did I want to say one last time to my mother? Then it dawned on me that I needed a Bible. I couldn't believe I didn't even think to bring mine with me. I walked to the nurses' station and asked if they could find a Bible for me. Theresa said they could probably bring one up from the chapel downstairs.

While I waited for Theresa to return with the Bible, I called Carol to see if she wanted to say goodbye.

"Hi. I'm at the nursing home. Mom is failing, and the nurses don't think she will make it through the night. Are there any last words you'd like to share with her? She's unconscious, but she still might hear you through the fog."

"Oh. There are probably a hundred things to say to her, but I can't seem to think of them now. You know, you rehearse this moment time and again in your mind. Now that the time is here, how do you put it all into a few words?"

"I know exactly what you mean. The words are the last she will hear from us. What is most important to say?"

"Okay. Just give me a few minutes and I will call back on Mom's phone, and you can hold it up to her ear. Does that work?"

"Yes. That's perfect."

Before Carol called back, Theresa entered Mom's room and handed me a Bible. While she was there, she checked Mom's vitals again. They were about the same. I told Theresa that my sister was going to call to say her goodbyes and then I was going to read some scripture to Mom.

"I believe she will hear you. There is no medical proof that comatose people can hear, but I believe they can.

I've seen patients improve when their loved ones come to visit. Spend as much time with her as you wish."

"Thanks again for everything," I said as Theresa left the room and pulled the door closed as she left.

The phone rang with Carol's call. I answered and held the phone to Mom's ear. Carol said a few things to Mom and then prayed the Lord's Prayer. I told her I would call when I heard from the nursing staff that she was gone. Carol was crying as we hung up the phone.

I turned to Mom and opened the Bible.

"I'm not really sure what are your favorite Bible verses, so I will share mine with you. I think I'll start with Psalm 23. Everyone likes Psalm 23, and most people have it memorized. I remember in the second grade when we had to memorize it, and I still remember it today." I knew I was rambling, but if Theresa was right and Mom could hear me…

I read a few other psalms while I was in that book: Psalm 46, Psalm 91, and Psalm 100. From there, I read Jeremiah 29 and Lamentations 3. I read the entire Romans 8 (my very favorite book and chapter of the Bible). I read some from John 17, Ephesians, and Philippians. Having exhausted my favorite Scripture verses, I took Mother's hand in mine and prayed for her. During the entire time, I didn't break down and cry. My voice was strong, and I knew the words I wanted to say.

Theresa came in again around 9:00 p.m. to check vitals again.

"Wow. It looks like she has made some improvement."

"Really? Is that a good sign?"

"Well, it's always good when their vitals improve, but I think it's probably just because you are here. She senses your presence and hears what you've been saying to her. Unfortunately, it probably won't last more than a couple of hours. By the way, I just wanted you to know that the snow is getting heavier. I know you have a distance to drive. I'm not saying you have to leave. I just wanted you to know."

"Thank you for the information. I don't think we will be staying much longer." Turning again to Mom, I just started talking to her as if she really was lucid.

"Did you hear Theresa? The roads are starting to get worse. We will have to leave in a little while. You know, Mom, it's okay for you to go too. You don't have to stay here for me. I know you've wanted to go home for months, and now you have a chance. Heaven wasn't exactly what you had in mind, but I think heaven is going to look just like Florida to you. There will be sunshine and warm weather, no snow. I know how much you hate the snow. The first person to greet you will be Jesus, but just think of the others you will see as well. Your mom and dad will be there. I know you had troubled relationships with them, but you will finally be happy to see them. All the heartache will be gone. There won't be any more animosity or hard feelings. You'll just be happy to sit with them and catch up. Your brother, Louis, will be there too. You haven't seen him since you were a young girl. The two of you will have so much to catch up on! You will also get to see Irv and Marge, Evelyn and Bill. So many people there are going to be excited to see you! You have so much to look forward to. You don't want to waste your time here languishing in this bed. Although I'll be sad for a time when you leave, I know you will be in a much better place. You will finally find peace and joy, two things I believe eluded you here on Earth. Please, don't worry about me. I'll be just fine. I called Carol and told her what was happening. She has been praying for you as well. She also sends her blessing for your next adventure. Say hello to everyone when you get to heaven. I will be rejoicing in your reunion."

The clock displayed 10:00 p.m. I kissed Mom's forehead and told her goodbye. As Ben and I walked to the car, the tears finally came. The snow fell faster as we carefully made our way north. The drive was slow going, and I was exhausted when we arrived home. I collapsed into bed and said a final prayer for Mom.

"Take good care of her, Lord. Make her passing easy, and give her that final peace that passes all understanding."

EPILOGUE

Through the fog of sleep, I heard my cell phone ring. I had put it on the bedside table before going to bed. I just had a hunch. Blurrily, I looked at the alarm clock, 2:30 a.m. I knew who was calling before I even answered. The night nurse on duty at St. Margaret Hall was calling to tell me that Mother was gone. I thanked her for calling and sat on the edge of the bed. A mixed bag of emotions hung around my neck as my life with Mom played through my mind like a silent film. It was finally over. I wish I could say that I was sad, and I do believe there was a part of me that was. Mostly, I felt relieved. This must be how a boxer feels when he steps from the ring after a match. I didn't have to fight anymore.

I called my sister. It was only 10:30 p.m. in Alaska, and I hoped she might still be up. She was. When I told her, she cried. Once she began crying, my own tears finally found their escape. Neither of us cried because Mother had died. We cried because of all the unrealized potential, all the unlived dreams, all the missed opportunities that died with Mother that night. Her life could have been so much more, held so much more love, enjoyed so many more close relationships, found so much more joy—if only she could have let go of her bitterness and pettiness.

My sister always said our mother taught us how to live by her negative example. Neither of us wanted to be like Mom. But because of Mom's example, we loved our families every day, we showed kindness to others, we valued truth and honesty, and we loved our God. It would have been awesome to have received those gifts from her in love instead of through her negativity, but Carol and I remain to this day thankful that we did not pass that on to our children and our grandchildren. We were able to teach by a better example.

The next morning, I tried to call Uncle Ray to let him know, but I could get no answer at his house. He didn't have a cell phone, so the landline was the only way to reach him. Finally, I tried my cousin's cell phone. He answered after a couple or rings. The reason Uncle Ray didn't answer the phone was that he was in the hospital. I told my cousin I would stop by the hospital after I visited the funeral home, but he told me not to come right then. The doctors and nurses said Uncle Ray would probably be home by the weekend, and I could come see him then.

Ben and I went to the funeral home to finish Mother's final arrangements. The director allowed us to "visit" with Mom for a few minutes. The first thing I noticed was her face. I knew by the look on her face that she had seen Jesus. She was finally at peace. My heart swelled with joy.

On Sunday, I called my cousin again as I thought it would be a good day to visit, but he wouldn't give me any definite time. He said Uncle Ray had taken a turn for the worse, and it wasn't a good time. My gut told me I should go to the hospital anyway, but I respected the family's wishes. I called my cousin again on Monday to say I really wanted to see Uncle Ray. When my cousin answered the phone, he was crying. Uncle Ray had just died five days after his sister. I cried. I didn't get to say goodbye, to tell him I loved him one more time. My heart was broken into more pieces. At least, the brother and sister were together again with the rest of the family. Peace be with you, Uncle Ray.

Mom, I know you hate this book. What would the neighbors think? I can hear your voice as I write. However, now that you are resting in the arms of Jesus, I hope you can see that I wrote this book to try to help others not to fall into the traps and pitfalls that we endured. Whether you believe it or not, the book was written with love.

Diane

www.ingramcontent.com/pod-product-compliance
Lightning Source LLC
LaVergne TN
LVHW041809060526
838201LV00046B/1186